driendl*architects

Ritual/Original

Park Books

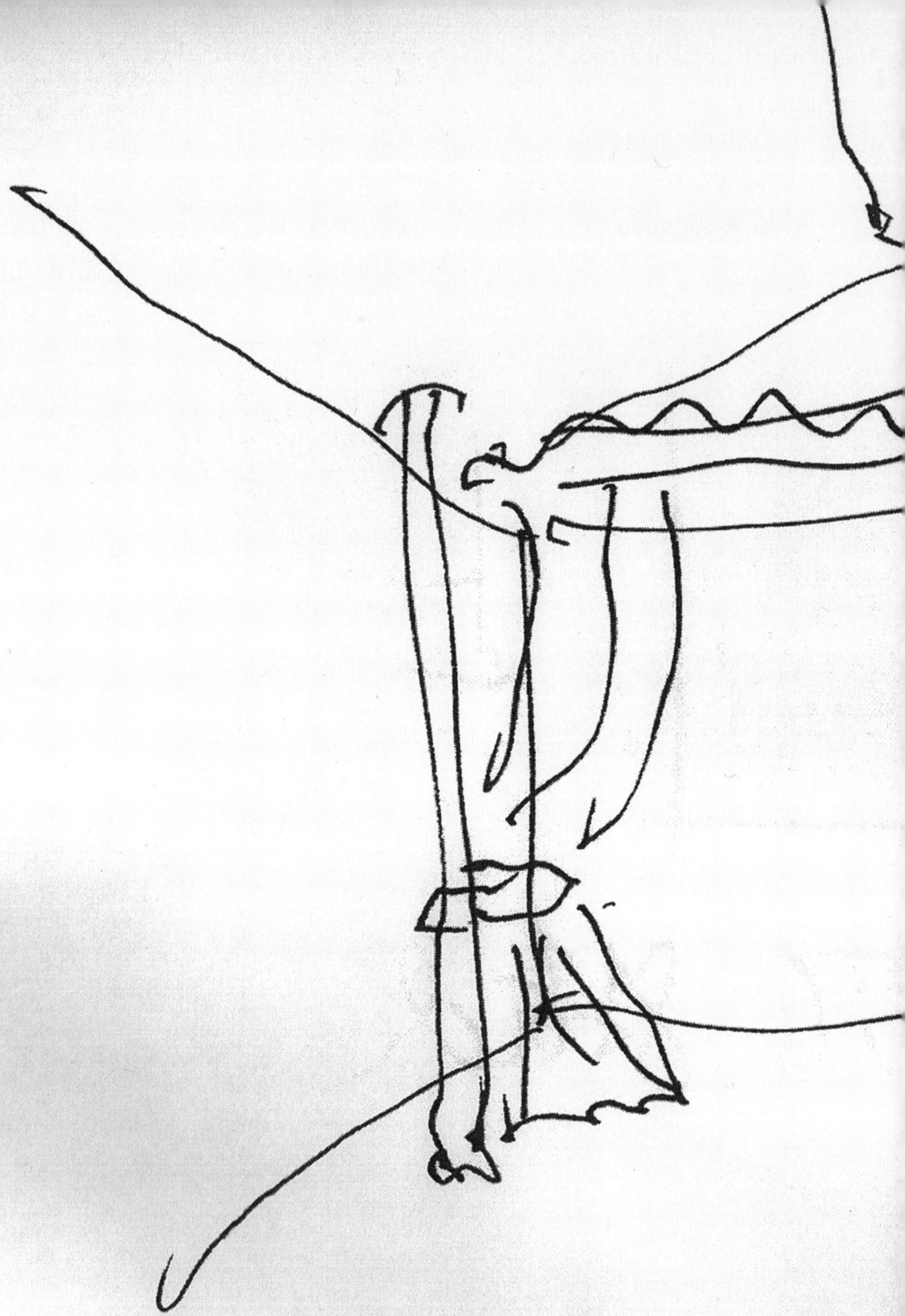

0

Imagination

Imagine that nobody imagines, and no one is left standing there before you with empty hands, then we are rid of the notion. Without imagination, the path simply continues on and on as before. Always in the same rut. Sometimes it just seems like something gets in the way. Actually, I usually get in my own way. It's like this: I carry my imagination in front of me so that which I envision sees only itself. Incidentally, carrying an idea around is hard enough, and hence the one doing the carrying loses strength when the vision is gone, and he or she is left standing there with no idea whatsoever. It's tedious to keep a vision unabatedly exciting and to set aside the highly interesting, motivated, politically correct, social, and imaginative aspiration of lasting value. When what you think is to remain concealed—or if what you think finds expression—it stands before you, hence it presents itself to you, and has thus already been introduced. So why all the effort? Position yourself, at best beforehand. We live in a world of those at the front. What if we imagine what should be, and all of a sudden it is?

overconfidence is the determiner
the li'l sausage to the big sausage:
when I need something, I don't go to the blacksmith'l, I go to the blacksmith
the philosopher to the pioneer:
if you want recognition, leave out the "l" at the end of your name
now we are d*a

drien
d*a
driendl*architects
d*a
driendl*architects

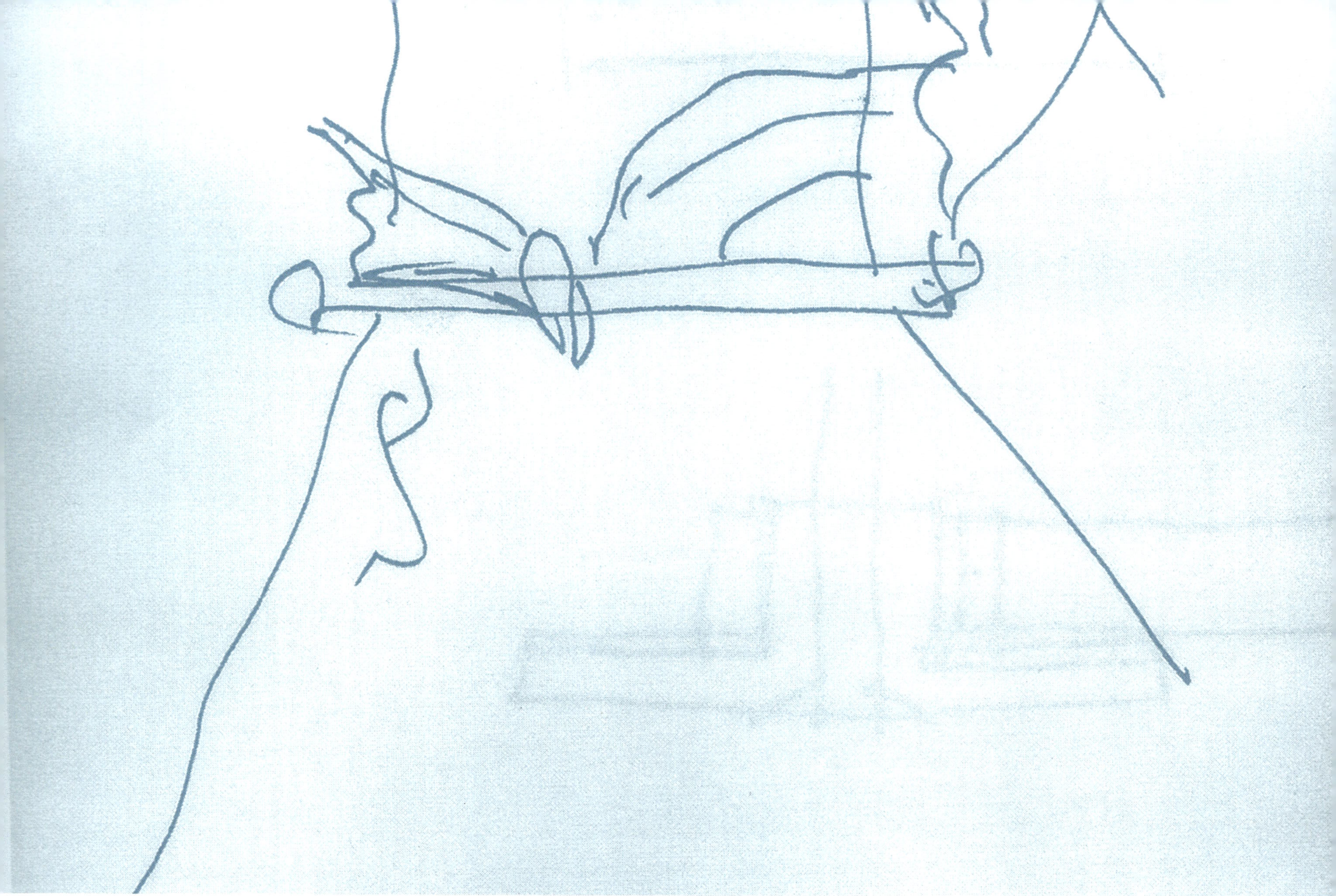

good night good morning good afternoon good day good for the moment
to and fro and back and forth and over and again and thus and why and exactly and above and beyond and pronto
and never and disappear

I don’t want to continue anymore
not just like this
or even as punishment
nothing written
falsely written
said and done
said something
something done
nothing lost
done everything
initially
new
with and without
nice
could be

it doesn’t work anymore
I can’t take any more
I don’t know any more
how should that work?
what’ll happen?
it’ll work out

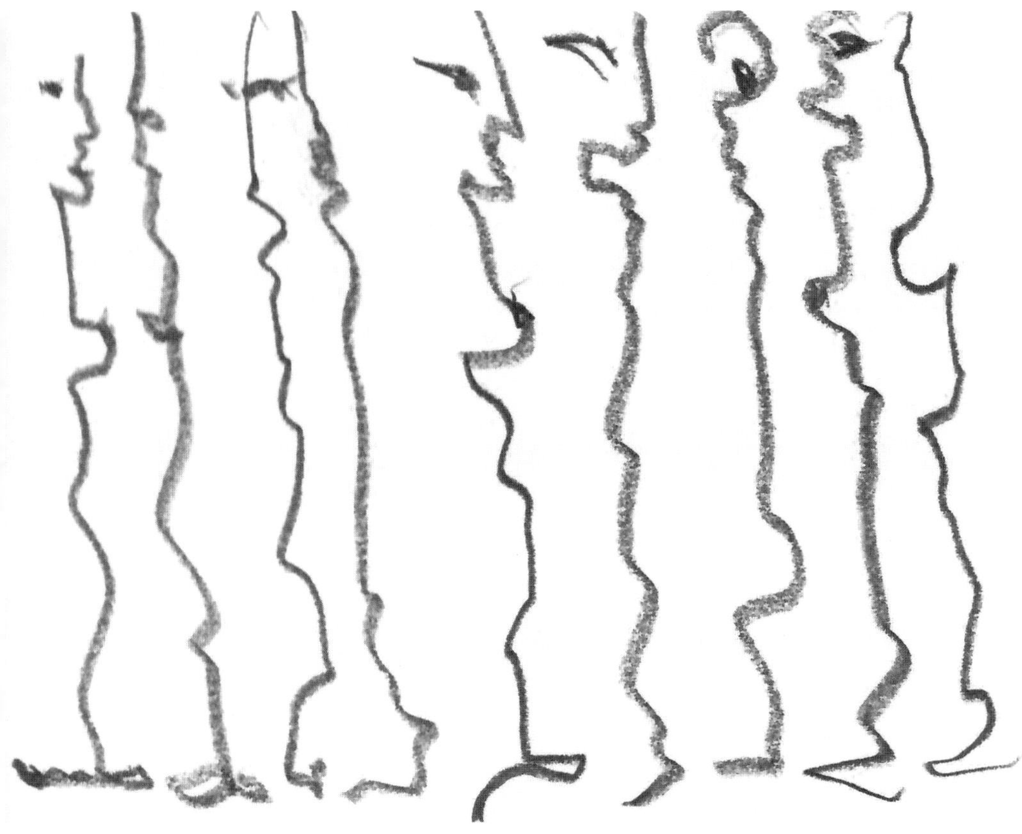

where is it?
I gave it to you
no
oh yes, definitely
I can't remember
it was with all the files
no, I would remember that
sure it was there. where did you put it?
everything is here in this spot
it's not there
so you didn't give it to me
yes I did. wait, maybe I took it with me after all
where are the new files?
here
yeah, here it is

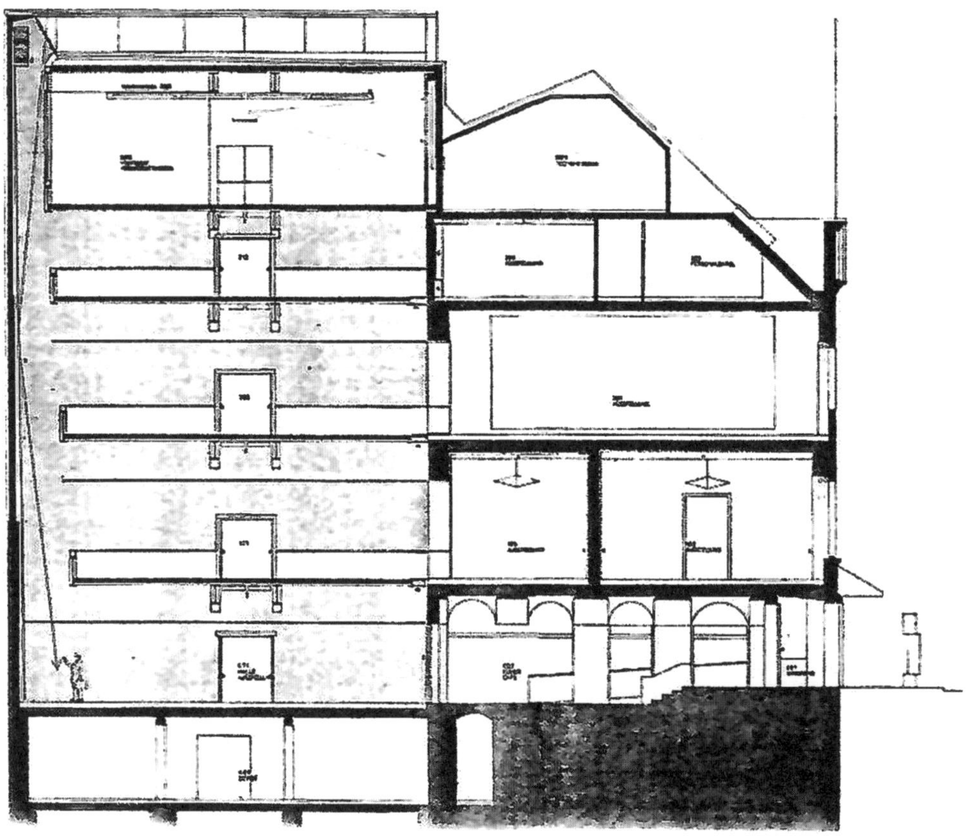

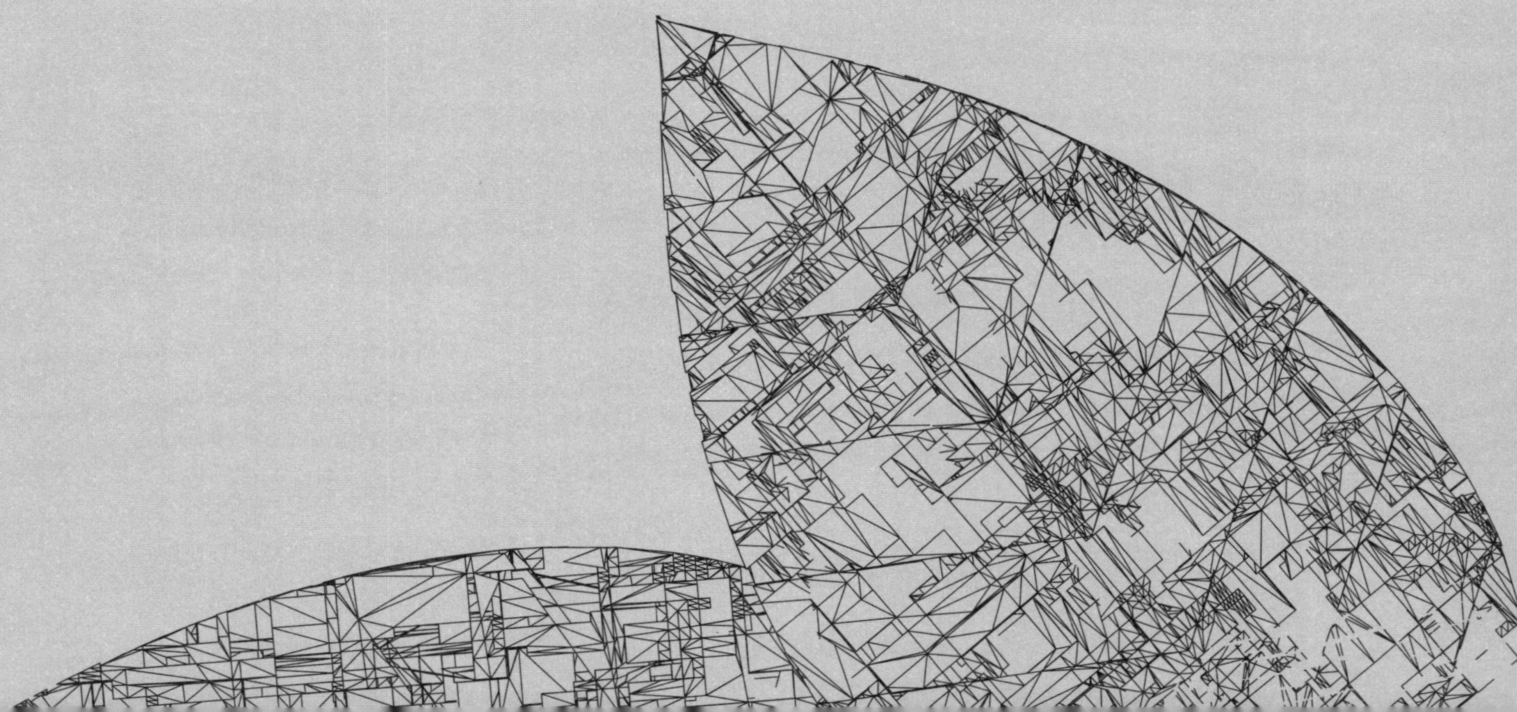

iHouse

Andrea, come take a look
a house for commerce
a house for production
a house for politics
a house for God
a house for gatherings
a house for guests
a house for art
a house for sports
my house for you

awready

thatahgen

notdateeder
Idonbleevit
wontworkaniwaze
notahgen

hekantdoodat
aintneither
Idonbleevdat
nah

yoodonhaviteether
yooainiteether
notdatway
with

despitedat, widat, widme
foryooforever
livwitluv

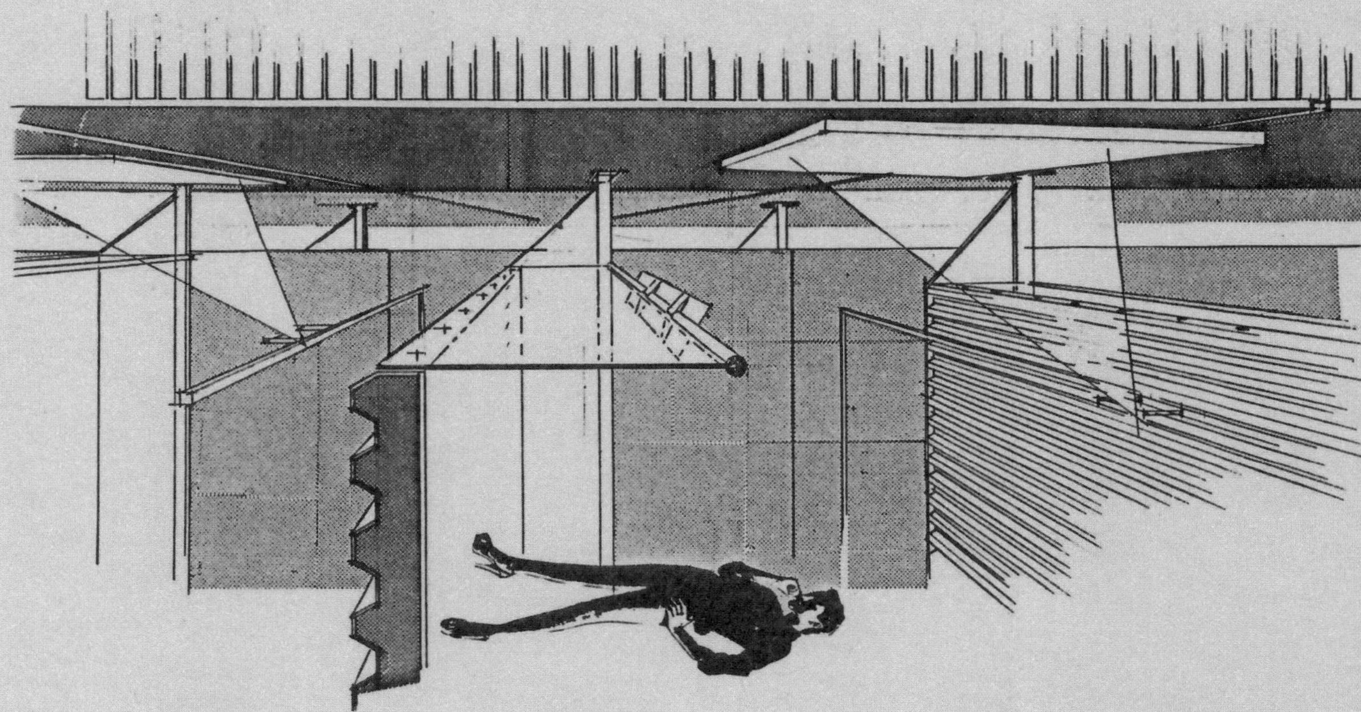

```
a hat, a cane, an umbrella,
a house, a table, a chair, a bed, and
forwards, backwards, sideways - stop!
one and two and three and four and
five and six and seven and eight
for whom, why, and what and where,
how did we do that?
```

... yes, how did we do that, for whom, why, what and why?

Twenty years of driendl*architects and the urge to link the practical work on projects with ideas that touch us, and to share all this in an old-fashioned way, appear to us to be good reasons for an airy condensation put to paper. The built thoughts, the people, and the systems that unmistakably affect us again and again are allowed here to interact with the visible. In this venture we are guided by two fundamental thoughts: We are all permanently situated in a built environment, or we are confronted with it, and so we* dare to begin by establishing the following: Architecture is not architecture and architecture is not by architects. Architecture is always related to the people who use it; it is influenced by them and vice versa. The necessary is linked to a concrete idea via imagination that ultimately brings the material into form, then there is a thing, a space, a path ...

All our imagined ideas grow into visions through the analysis of existing strategies, structures, and conditions. Ideally, some of these visions are implemented experimentally here and there in real surroundings. The big challenge is to find a consensus with the idea and a positive effect for the users. Of course, the physical act of building is not an experiment. The protective roof must not fall on the heads of the people who trustingly seek refuge beneath it. Nevertheless, as history shows, it remains a continual process of repeated experimentation, in which each time we ask ourselves again what invisible laws make a significant contribution to whether and how a project is realized and what traces it leaves behind.

Viewed from the other side, however, something built is an intervention that entails change, ideally improvement. On this matter we dare to argue: All matter is air displacement, dynamically by means of movement, statically by delimitation, and chemically by combustion. Architecture will, in this sense, always be "displacement of air through matter." The matter is the shell. That which the matter envelops, delimits, is the airspace newly created for our purposes. We are making it the focus of our attention, and from this frame of reference we see the most essential task for the future: architecture without air pollution—architecture of air. A vision—reality desired?

These are just a few of the reflections we have had in the course of our exploratory journey. During this time, however, we have also learned something important: with all seriousness and necessity, there must also be instances of the beautiful, the great, the funny, and the flawed, because smiling about yourself and of course joy(!) form a counterweight that relativizes and holds everything in balance. This encourages us to explore further.

With this in mind, we heartily invite you to continue this perhaps somewhat peculiar round dance, to find more and even more, to smile with us, to marvel, to hope, and finally to ask what traces we want to, will, and should leave behind ...

And now: Raise the curtain! Voilà! The cult that lies behind—from the vision to the symbiosis with the purpose, to the matter, and then the salvation of our imagination, and perhaps also a little paradise in the now for all—or is that too much to ask? Kathrin Turanitz

*The "we" in the text encompasses not just all those who have contributed to making this book, but also family members and many friends, regardless of their partisan affiliations or religious interests.

1

The Invisible

The relationship between skin and fabric sizzles, be it scratchy or smashing, soothing or irritating, it is at any rate invisible; it simulates a positive influence on the robustness of the intimacy of the thus protected ego—it is simply more resilient. The finest sensuous materiality offers security in its diffusion and implicitness. Similarly, supposed flaws can be elegantly compensated and ameliorated, even without surgical cuts. In other words, underwear fulfills the function of social compensation. It creates an idealized image and the ability to prevent problems with the appearance and density of that which emerges. The highly unjust capriciousness of nature is brought into line and, beyond that, heat, cold, moisture, odor, and even radiation and conception are regulated. Quality in the choice of underwear is, at any rate, a decisive factor in maintaining a commensurate appearance.

justice, measure, law – godly, human

1. devoid of self-interest
satiated, healthy, and not on slippery ice

2. driven by an inner urge
endowed with talent for art – up front

3. with no external pressure
man is born free, yet everywhere he is in chains

media person

a 29-year-old proposition: the internet
aspire to the hit parade of high culture
put on the net
general availability and retrievability
information
interpretation
global avant-garde
trendsetters
inflation
form via visual communication
comment without filter
culture without background
ego
explosive subject
self-fulfillment model
unguided private
common good?
social commitment?
competent secondary matter
surface
iconoclasm?
iconoclastic controversy?
turning point
global culture war!

LOFTS
Panofsky DÜRER
PIRANESI
HOME
LONDON STYLE
Richtig reisen
THE AGE OF CAPITAL
COLLECTED STORIES
the mesh
Technische Analyse
Meine Danziger Mission
LONDON
AMERICAN HOUSE NOW
Paris Apartments
HEXENJAGD
WHAT'S MINE IS YOURS
EINE ANATOMIE DER MACHT
HABIT
CHARLES DUHIGG
PHYSIK
FREUD
RECHT
ARCHIV

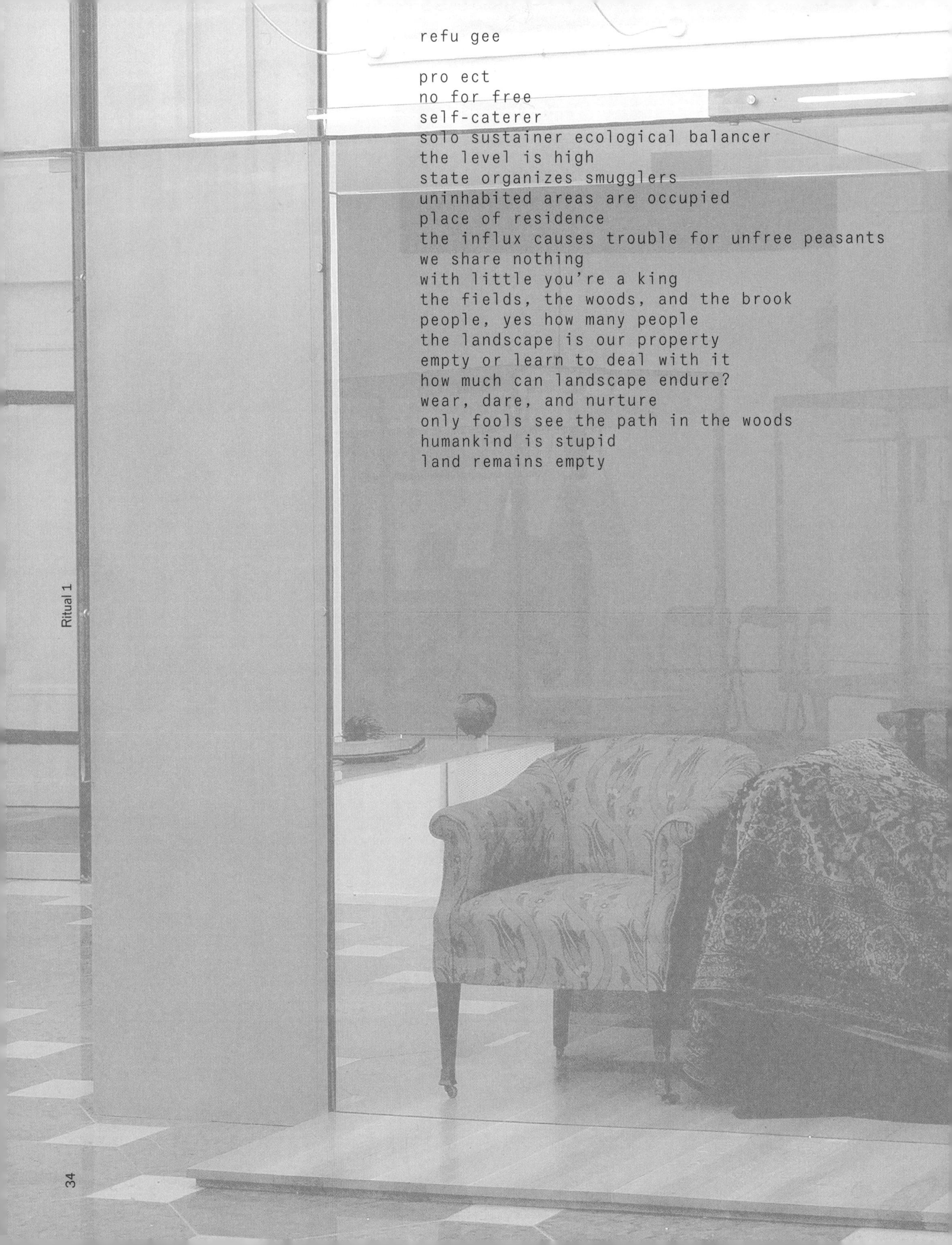

refu gee

pro ect
no for free
self-caterer
solo sustainer ecological balancer
the level is high
state organizes smugglers
uninhabited areas are occupied
place of residence
the influx causes trouble for unfree peasants
we share nothing
with little you're a king
the fields, the woods, and the brook
people, yes how many people
the landscape is our property
empty or learn to deal with it
how much can landscape endure?
wear, dare, and nurture
only fools see the path in the woods
humankind is stupid
land remains empty

Studie, auf die man sich beziehen könnte
und sagen: „Hier ist ein definitiver

LOFTS
NIALL FERGUSON
AMERICAN HOUSE NOW
Paris Apartments
ADORNO SCHRIFTEN 7
EINE ANATOMIE DER MACHT
DA VINCI
HEXENJAGD
DUBROVNIK
THE GREAT SEA
THE FREEMASONS

stance

legal construct
ordinances
regulations
conventions
laws
traditions
principles
standards
watch out!

building onward

a glance at the clock abide adjust agree alter argue ask assemble be amazed be annoyed be certain be thankful believe block break off burrow calculate check clarify collaborate combine communicate comprehend conceptualize consider construct contemplate contend dare decide delight develop discard discern discontinue disturb dream encourage enquire err establish evince fight back find get to know go hold hope imagine insist juggle kick-start laugh learn lend an ear let go listen monitor no notice observe open order organize participate pass on present quarrel recall receive renew rethink review say see settle shake your head sketch someone speak square stand stop submit surprise teach think along think critically think things through tidy up travel here travel there try understand vacate weigh wonder x y z …

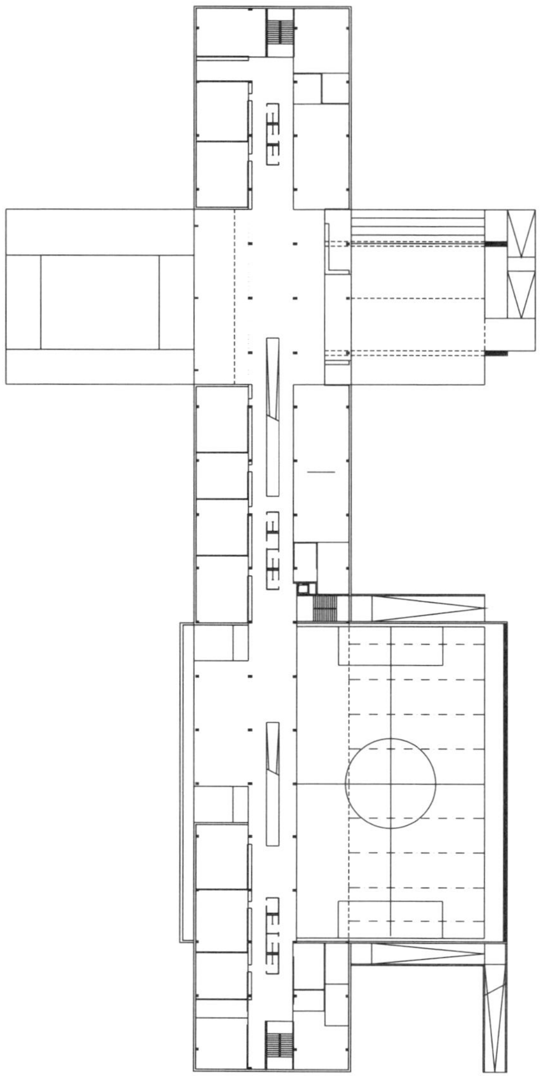
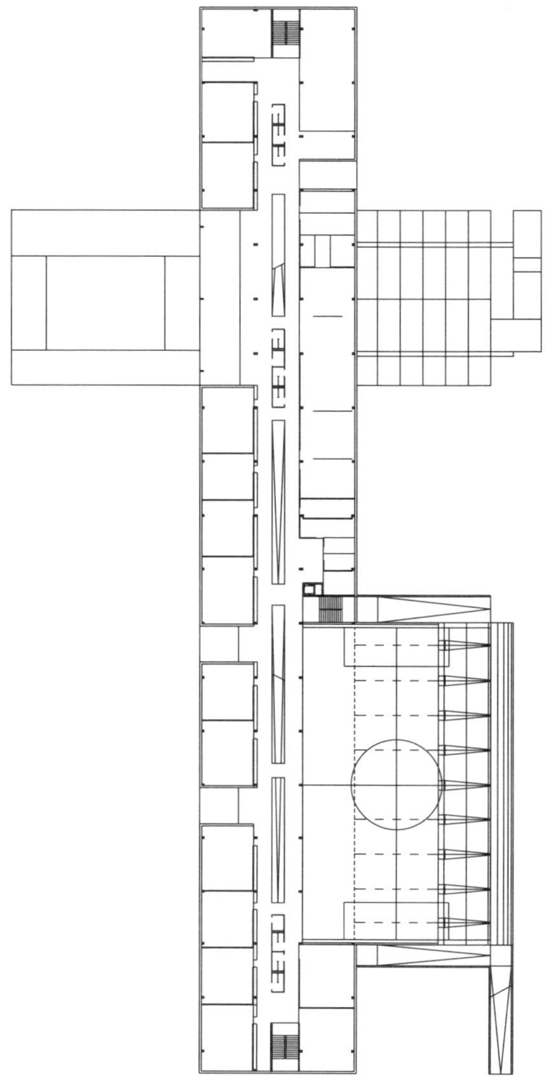
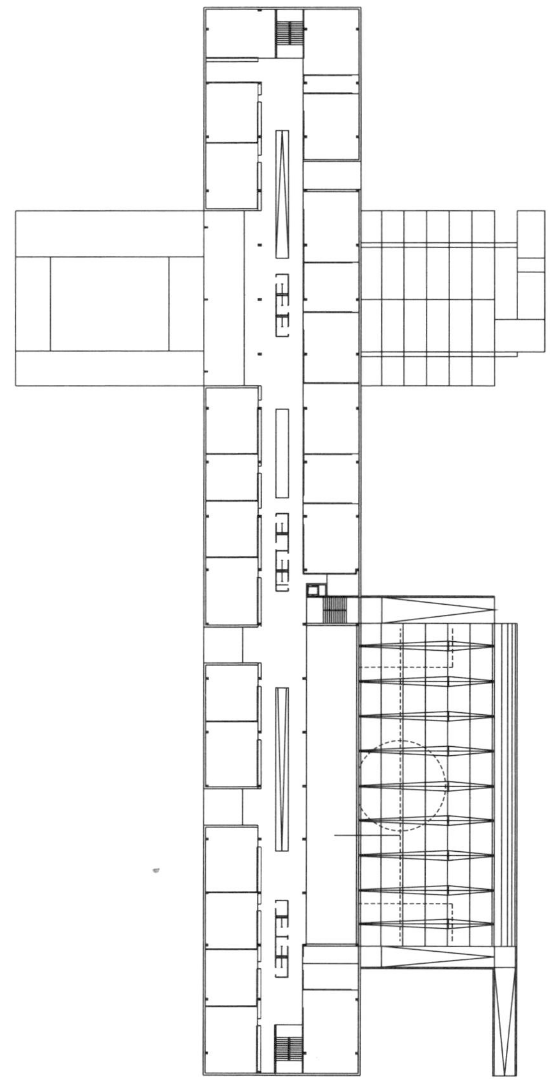

senses

faced with so many, each does everything and nothing
discourse is lacking
what makes sense?

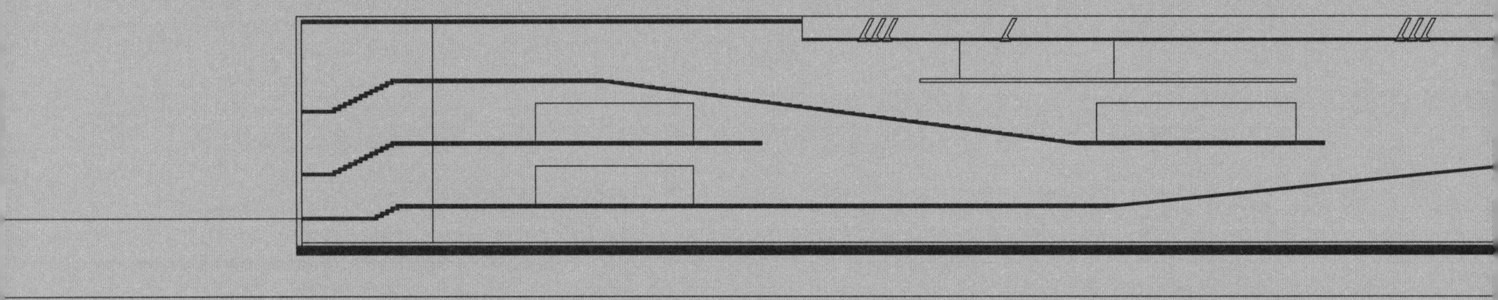

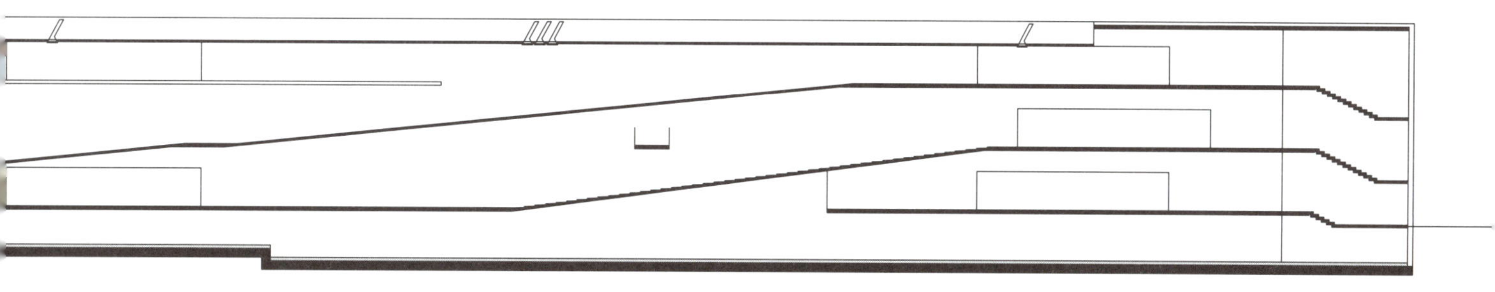

nice to eat

ingredients
air and water
a little bit grubby but at least temporarily
available almost everywhere

oh fruits
in the winter when it's bitterly cold
the fresh grapes from south africa sweeten the gloomy days
and provide solace

nuts
beans
ancient grains
fairly traded this way and that

fish
snail mussels
game
frog eggs
swarms of insects and birds that can't fly
sheep cattle swine
kept in animal-friendly conditions

for good eating
luxurious privilege
state guarantee for worry-free consumption

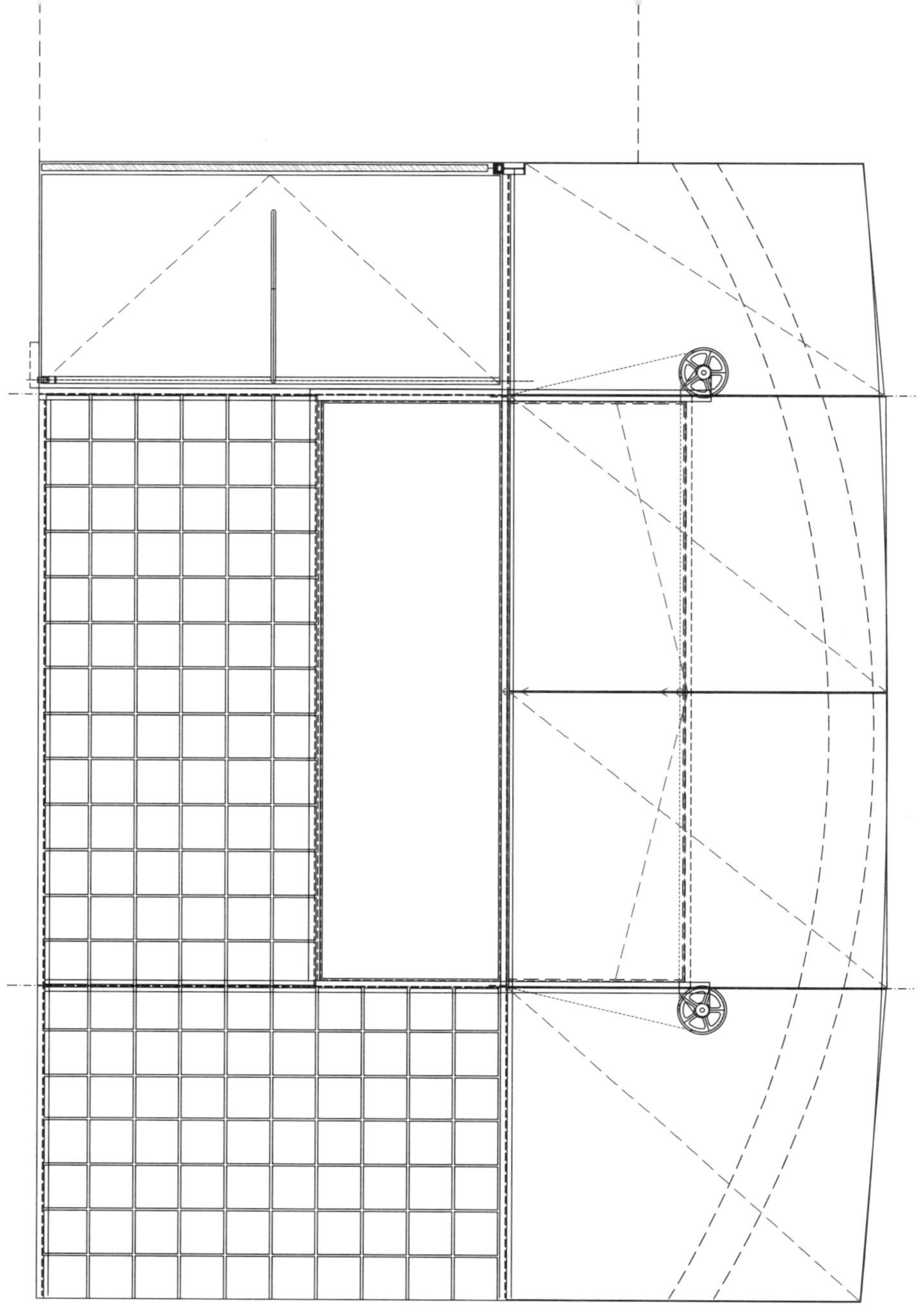

Learning

The right to education. The right to ignorance. The right to nudity. The right to equality.

"We're playing school, and you're the teacher—no, I'm the teacher! Today's program: We'll cut out figures with scissors, but it's dangerous. No, no, you don't know how to do that. I'll do it. Where did you learn that? I just can and you can't. Reading, writing, and arithmetic, at least, and then maybe the entire history of grown-ups, oh God! Lazy, hard working, talented, skillful, attentive, clever—all thrown into the classroom so they, the teachers, can tastefully present the boring stuff. Yeah, real life; you'll see. Something or other is going wrong, something isn't right, there's something in the air, we already suspect it, growing up won't be so easy; you just have to press on regardless and how long it takes, uh-oh! Even though we already know everything so much better than the teachers, they have to struggle with us students and don't exactly notice that we're actually already adults. We're only in school because nobody has time at home, but that doesn't make it any better. School: it's not that bad—kinda like being at home with the sisters ..."

Cut

Frontal teaching, the sexes are segregated, also for sports, healthy exercise. In my schooldays it was called physical education; the equipment smelled of cold sweat and looked terrifying. Torture chambers. Add to that the gym teacher's strict commands and critical gaze to ensure the correct sequence and proper stance. Everyone line up in a row! All are prepared for life as links in a chain ...

Excursus

a: Did you dream something?
b: Yes, a wish has come true.
a: Well, which one?
b: Stupid question; of course he was already gone!

```
thought,
doubt
education,
delusion,
iconoclasm
```

What do we think? How do we think? I think, therefore I am. Am I also if I don't think—if I only am? Who thinks?

It is said there are three types of thinking: in spoken and written words, in images, and in patterns—so we are told (discovered by modern researchers). In fact, they are forms of artistic expression or of artistic creation. It has nothing to do with thinking. One could also add the artistic: thinking in numbers, thinking in relationships, conceited thinking, underhanded thinking. The process of thinking is actually irrelevant. In my opinion there is absolutely no evidence that man ever thinks anything except what he needs to consider day in and day out. If "deducing" can even be accepted as a way of thinking at all. Here we have learned to choose from various possibilities of expression: dancing, singing, writing, reading; the whole shebang. Today, some apps help out too. Initial proof of thinking would be to stop knocking out sayings—that acquired art of overtaxing language to such an extent and of writing it down as text in such labyrinthine referential systems and cross-references that centuries will be needed to decipher these special constructs—and instead say something that has not been uttered and needs to be said. And to say it in such a way that the receiver—that is to say, the one to whom that which is said should say something, and also understand what has been said, without any previous education, delusion, or other excuses. What is meant with what is said is text, language, music, imagery, technology, etc. When feelings come into play, the thinking stops or we are told: please stop thinking! Everyone knows that, in love as in pain. The fact that we are not always in love or constantly plagued by pain makes us wonder what would happen if these conditions lasted forever. We forget that everything else around us thinks as little as we do.

We are, not because we think; we are because everything else is. What, besides love, pain, and hunger, constantly drives us to want to ponder things we don't understand anyway. Those who understand everything do not fall in love and, of course, as any Indian knows, know no pain. Maybe they are even monsters. That would mean that we should be very careful about thinking and, above all, not take it too seriously. Also because everything around us, like the weather, love, the forest, the sea, pain, mother, father, son, and daughter, could strive for eternal becoming if we do not one day forget where we came from. Every day something new is added to what has been said. We reinvent ourselves time and again. The Renaissance, imagined astray in the rearview mirror.

Paideia: We had learned to write ...
Renaissance: ... have become artists and scientists ...
WWW: ... now we know everything, every one of us.

And all that after a few thousand years of faltering development! It's incredible how quickly we have realized that information and communication should be accessible and available directly and without barriers, to anyone and everyone at all times. We simply need to learn how this miracle works—especially how everyone in every circumstance can reach the transformer that connects us to the central unit and makes the exchange possible. At the moment the flow is still a bit halting, the transformer is not yet part of the body; the synapses will be homely, stress-free spaces in a protective, unhampered atmosphere. Everyone has access, that's the prerequisite.

Teaching, training, studying—at home, in a building, in an institution. Since general education has for many generations become compulsory for all children and law for governmental societies, substance and form are nearly standardized and frozen, not only concerning the material to be taught, but also the mode of conveyance and the venue. In the political wrangling surrounding this hotspot, one has recognized in passing not just well-meaning ideals, but also the eternal adherence to yesterday's content and to the militarily organized institutional character of the buildings used for this purpose. One has gained the impression that lawmakers, spurred by the fear of change, have advocated the notion of, as it were, a broad-spectrum antibiotic—namely of integrating the subject in such a way that the perspective, in consideration of the social pyramid, has been directed primarily toward linear consolidation and continued existence. These tradition-conscious and conservation-minded dealings were secured democratically, by fear. This fear has been elaborated in education, perhaps quite unconsciously; here the circle comes to a close. Today we must increasingly discern that, if we allow a gap to form in our laws on education and the obligations they set out, what arises from this point of view is a right to dilettantism. We have agreed that everyone should learn to read, write, and do arithmetic in order to move about in society with as few barriers as possible once they reach adulthood. At the same time, however, we are so far advanced that meanwhile we can only hand over the legacies we have accumulated to a highly developed team of experts. Woe betide us if our offspring don't accept the job! Those coming after us won't have a carefree life anymore. Hence boundless education is our chance to take the bull by the horns; a new planet is not in sight—other misleading and soporific images are not productive.

We have meanwhile reached a technical stage of development that puts us in a position to give our planet Earth a different face and, in the process, to incidentally pull the carpet that's indispensable for our lives out from under our feet. That would be the end of the Anthropocene. Humanism has taught us how to interact with one another, but not until and only when it pertains to all. Now it has also become clear that our technical development must first learn how to deal with everything else. We don't have much time. We know that.

In a male-dominated atmosphere, technical skill and a sense of organization help the technician to leverage his propensity for mass enterprise (freely based on Karel Čapek: War with the Newts). A breach in this domain forces a disruption of the system with uncertain outcome.

Wars become more frequent and more brutal, with victims on all continents; focused terror targets individual subjects. As a signal of progressiveness, no more peoples are wiped eradicated, epidemics are banished temporarily where they are not needed, mature collectives are destroyed, and no one would have to die of hunger. Countermeasures seem hopeless, unimportant, and ominously bathed in a pallid light. The goal is reorientation, upheaval. No revolution, no counterrevolution, and no crisis but a worldwide shift. And we're afraid of that. This fear and the lethargic rigidity that accompanies it do not entitle us to stand by and watch idly and certainly not to join in.

Our entire milieu is affected: the environment, our circle of friends, our consciousness, even our microbiome; that's right, even the previously unknown field, the invisible, the silent, the blind itch. We are hindered by the worldwide propagation of prejudice, fueled by the irresponsibility of the advertising providers of mass communication via social media. Our astonishment at the speed of the global spread of idiocy should not keep us from systematically incorporating the fundamental insights gained from our "volition to know all" about everyone and everything as a legal construct of universal rights empowered by parliament. If it were not for historical examples of networks where ideas have "gone viral" across great distances worldwide (like Christianity or Islam ... according to Niall Ferguson), even having done so without the technology of the Web, still more astonishment would be legitimate. However, since general use of the public Web without monopoly restrictions disrupts our democratic development, fair regulation should be established for the self-promotion of individual interests of a subject's will.

Education here means the development of a sensorium for this new age of the Anthropocene, far away from the stress-ridden educational building for the individual being. The time has come: We're all in the same boat ...

Of our own accord. Information helps the subject to recognize the enveloping swarm of the milieu, or to grasp its inclusive integration. The subject is disruption of the connection.

Utopia now?

We have agreed that children must be educated and why, and that there must be buildings and people to undertake this enterprise. Without external pressure, the child should discover, as in playing a game, that reading, writing, arithmetic, and social behavior will be important later on. In addition to empathetic people who impart knowledge, this naturally also includes an environment that supports as much as possible the needed concentration and ambiance, and which encourages people to understand space as a conducive microclimate in all its qualities. Here we must learn to make every conceivable effort to manifest these spaces of first encounter with knowledge and art, as well as the communication of what we should or should not do with them later, as some of the most important tasks in our society. To put it plainly: it does not suffice to publicly train staff and build anonymous buildings in which education is conducted if we want to afford a utopia in the present for the future.

Complications generally begin when children turn their backs on the offerings as they transition to adulthood and go their own ways, or when they are overburdened by the system and left behind. School must be a place for all who are not yet adults, a place they like, so that their own inclinations find favor. Romantic humanism perhaps, but I fear it's the only way. This means both the teacher and the learner must be able to establish a positive relationship with the setting, and the setting must, in turn, be able to cope with this demand. As we have discerned over the millennia, spaces and buildings formatively shape us to varying degrees, depending on how much time we spend there. So, is there any interplay? In language we find all the stuff that has accumulated in this regard: the chair in the classroom building, the umbrella organization atop the pillar model, the time window next to the master plan. The material is not dead as long as it is in use, above all for its intended use. The first thing we ever learn is to sojourn in another house outside our parents' home. The first bit of interplay comes about through the comparison of being at home and in the other house. What's it like here, what's it like there? Besides experiencing that the other house is used by other people, we recognize the differences in the nature of the house. There are bigger rooms, different materials, other furnishings, and also different habits and customs. We adapt to the transient dialogue with the new house and the practices celebrated within it. Punctuality, that is probably the sharpest interrupting noise produced by ringtones, and it means that now something is starting or is finally over. The allocation of time and the attendant ability of changing places, fleeing them in a hurry, or, ashamed and mocked, entering them belatedly, is undoubtedly the safest fixation of an emerging subject to a specific place. This action is burned into us and becomes the matrix: off during recess, down the corridor and out into the open in the schoolyard, assuming the weather is decent. Order temporarily ceases to exist. Higgledy-piggledy, everyone with everybody, without rules, and sometimes even a scuffle leading up to …

Interplay

Back to the interplay between the built and the ceremony, or both with us. Apart from a few exceptions—when quick improvisation is needed in disasters, for example—things are built according to fixed rules. Social ceremonies and formal agreements are also conducted according to pre-planned rules, and here, too, a few exceptions exist when something unforeseen happens, like war or revolution. Once built, the building is finished and thus fixed. Its essence is singular subjective effort and then rigidity. A ceremony is a temporally repeatable sequence of predefined events and participating subjects. Its essence is its repeatability and duration. Thus, when effort with subsequent rigidity is caused by the need for repeatability and duration, or vice versa, what emerges is permanent rigidity, albeit with a slight oscillation between the past and the future. Duration and rigidity are not relevant in the present. Exactly this moment is worthy of being considered more precisely, because here the condition of the individual essentially does not play a role anymore—and everyone knows this moment:
the exception.

That must be our goal.

That's why we need schools. For now! Georg Driendl

2 Technology

The first step toward the technology we have developed was arguably the word itself. All the senses of our existence are, as if intoxicated, reinforced, modified, expanded, accompanied, surrounded, amplified and accelerated by technology in an extraordinary process that is irreversible, advancing solely in one direction and driven by something ever better, beyond all control. The sole surviving and constantly renewing principle is the destruction of nature. Observing this movement in real time gives us moral certainty. For technology, there is no limit. Everything is possible, everything is doable; nothing is new but continuously in motion. The ostensibly new repeats itself identically with other means, everything is still not yet accomplished. When technology is fully functional, we will not have to worry about anything anymore. Nevertheless, the questions remain: How much? Where are we headed? How long?

Nichtschwimmer
Wassertiefe 1,30m
5
5

4

stylish formalism
architecture today
glazed palette
irregularly perforated cube
camouflaged surface, concealed mass
car-centered free-form
free the form
form-free

LAUFEN VERBOTEN

Ritual 2

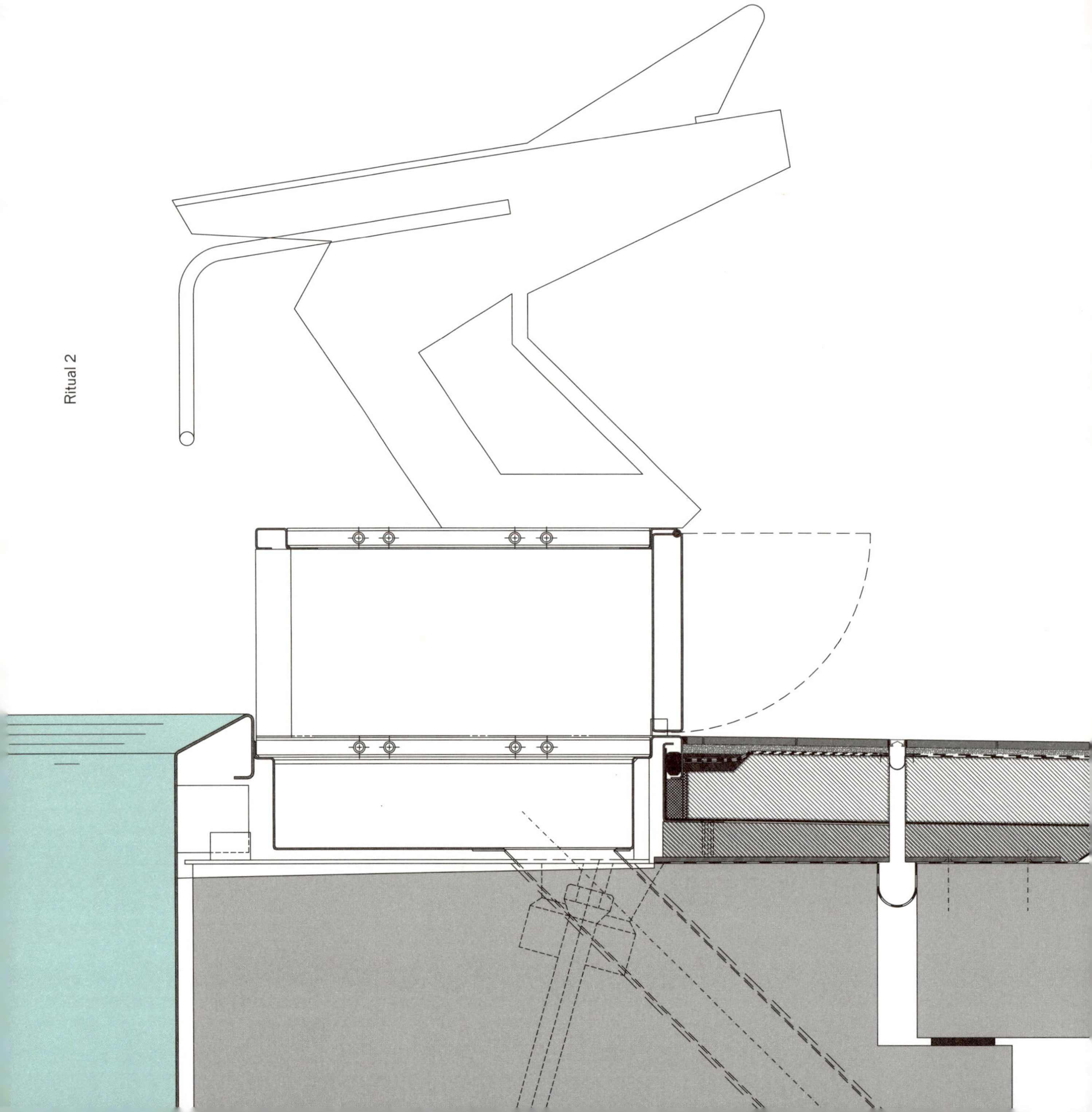

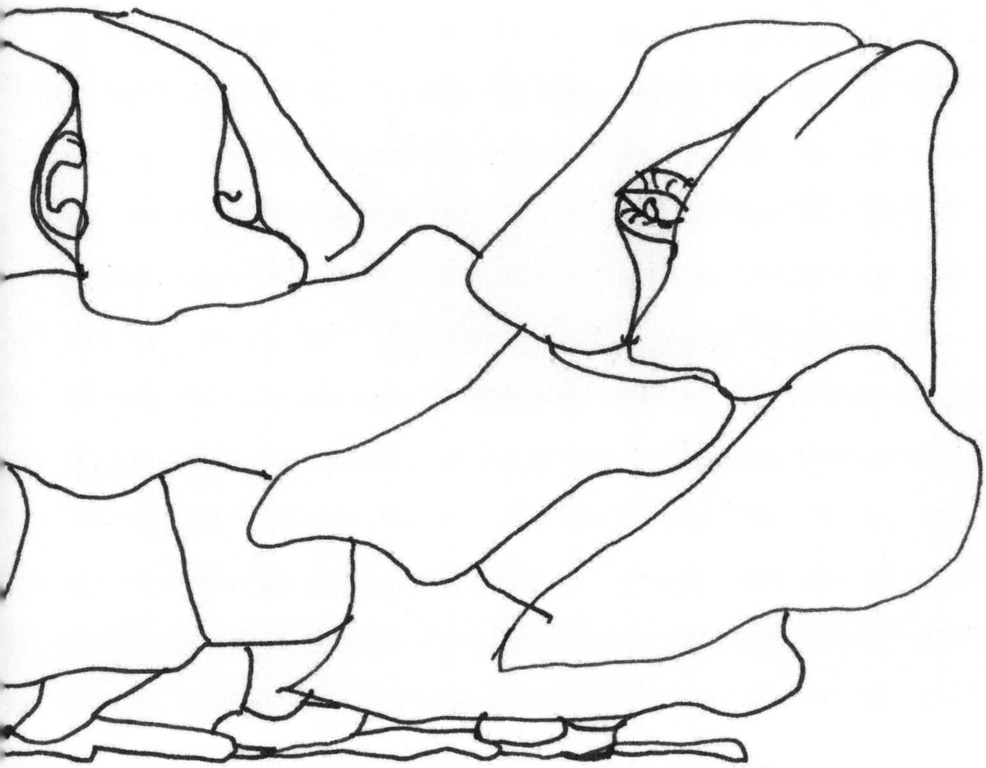

Ritual 2

“Then dismay all wisdom
from my soul disgorges”

Cicero

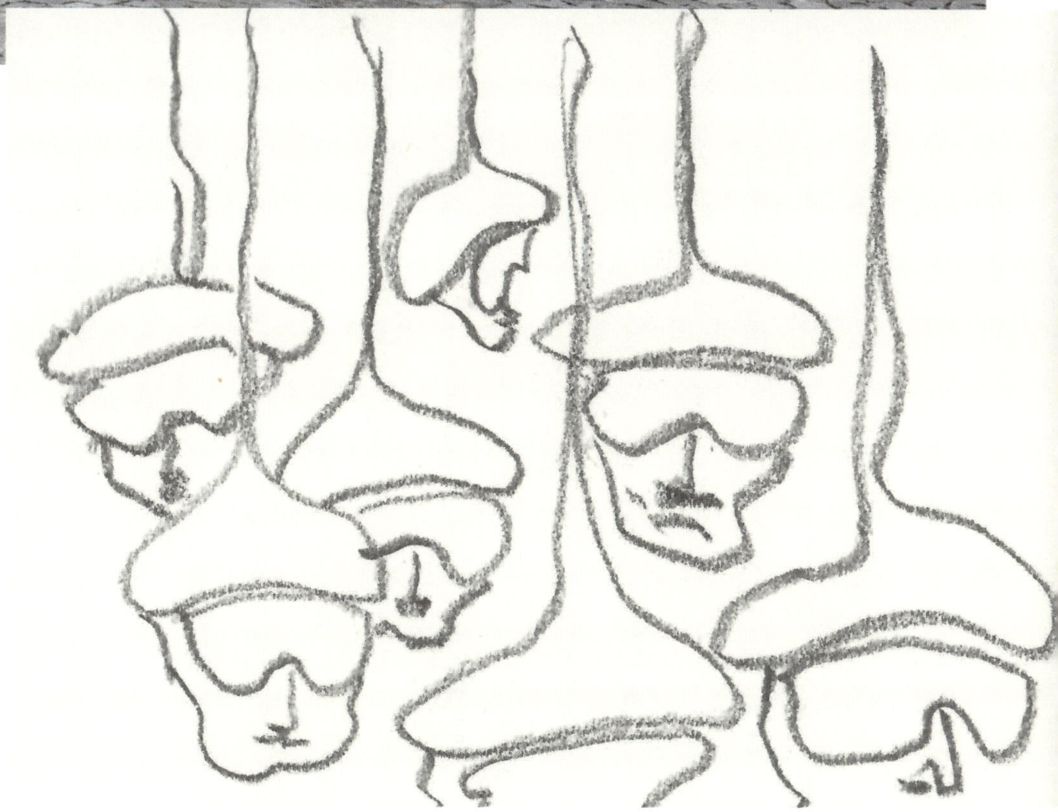

by the way
able
able stay
stay
able
stay by
by
the way

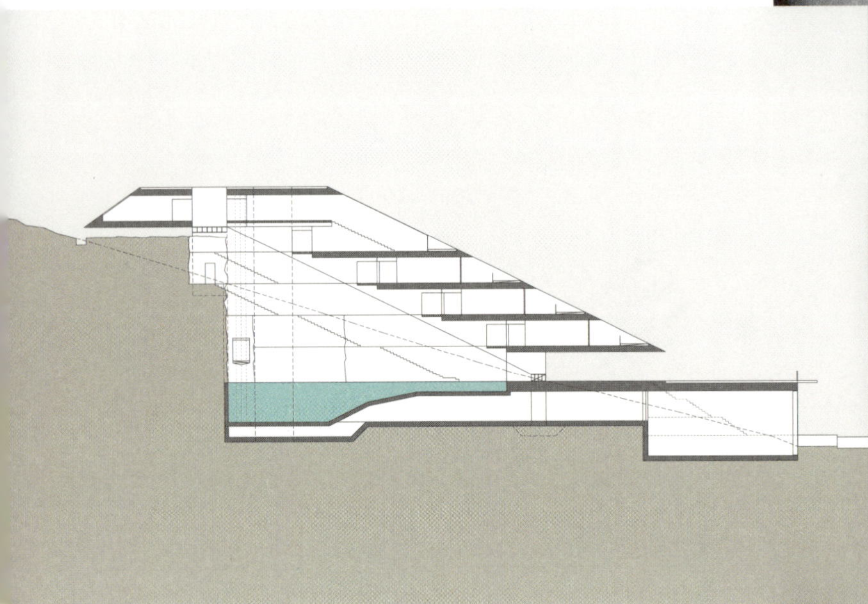

WELCOME, you JUMPERS ON FIFTEEN, it's SPRINGTIME at the SCHMELZ CEMETERY, WITH FRIENDLY ASSISTANCE, MODERN TIMES begin on the CATWALK of the TILE CITY. EVERYTHING TURNS BELLY-UP, even the HOUSING BUBBLE.

GOOD LUCK! for the PROTECTION OF HISTORIC MONUMENTS, welcome to the BALLET MÉCANIQUE for the CONSTRUCTION meeting; EVERYTHING here IS ILLUSION, even NATURE MORTE AVEC CLEANING HOSE, and GULLIVER'S TRAVELS come to an end. ORDER IS A MUST.

AVANTI POPOLO! across VERMILION and LEMON YELLOW, past NOCTURNAL WELD INSPECTIONS, POTEMKIN, the COURT-SWORN EXPERT, and the TURKISH SIEGE; all HOT AIR and safely NON-SLIP in the UNDERWORLD

SPLENDID BEES! WELCOME to the VIENNESE KITCHEN; TABLE DECK YOURSELF, the COCKROACHES are waiting for you, there are no RUTS, but at the EDGE OF THE PLATE is the SQUARE TO JUPITER AND SATURN.

THE POOR SKIN FEKETE, dressed in BLUE VELVET, awaits THE CONCIERGE IN THE COSMOS PARLOR

SHIP AHOY! a BENCH on the BEACH, LAST STOP SPEED for SUPER MARIO, no TECHNICAL JARGON, no ESCAPE, PUBLIC CONCERT in the WELLNESS AREA, long live ORGANIZATION!

STADTHALLENBAD

Construction

Some time ago, I had thoughtlessly accepted the invitation to give a lecture at a "Conversations for Change" event. I basically find it plainly ridiculous when, except for teaching or promotional purposes, architects present their own buildings—or even worse, what they would like to have built—under the guise of entertainment. Since the announcement listed the title "Sustainable Architecture" next to my name, although I hadn't been asked, I was able to use this emotive term to flee into the fashionable and usually misleading topic of sustainability.

Americans are working to colonize Mars, investing billions of dollars in this vision of the future. Should these plans of escaping into space one day succeed, all our worries in the here and now about the condition of our Mother Earth will have been in vain. Such goals show that our investigative mind explores scientifically, and that our perception of the "environment" reaches deep into microcosmic and macrocosmic space. In the rapid development of individual projects, their technical implementation has "positive" or "negative" effects on us.

Can growth be limitless? Can sustainability provide a solution? Or is it more of an ideal that we draw between technology, nature, society, and religion? The best-known attempt to manifest the concept of sustainability is that of the so-called three-pillar model, better known as the triple bottom line or 3BL, which calls for a well-balanced interplay of social, ecological, and financial aspects. This idealized model represents our desire to use slogans to create a harmonizing awareness—in this case, of our interaction with the environment. Unfortunately, important aspects are not taken into account; the angle of view is deliberately set too narrow.

The image of an onion—with a human being at its center and many layers that have grown over time—can serve us as an illustrative analogy: The outermost layer, or "shell," within which we subdue the earth and protect ourselves from nature, is formed by technology and construction. Peeling that back, the next layer comprises society and our social context, followed by yet another layer that is constituted by our clothing. Finally, we arrive at the most private layer, the shell closest to a person, which encompasses eating, drinking, and our ways of dealing with illness. Removing all these layers and shells leads directly to the self.

This line of reasoning raises the question of whether the slogan of "sustainability," as commonly used, is at all meaningful. After all, are the Egyptian pyramids sustainable just because they still exist and have withstood decay for thousands of years? They remain a physical presence, and for the time being at least, their sheer mass has meant that despite ruthless exploitation, the pyramids survive as symbols of a past culture. The society that created them no longer exists, nor does the knowledge behind their construction. So aren't the pyramids silent witnesses of social and societal erosion—long-lasting, misunderstood symbols of a former culture?

Following this argument, radioactive waste must be of uttermost sustainability: it will still occupy our thoughts and our lives even thousands of years from now. Although we have needed to cut down fewer forests in the service of energy production over the past few decades, we now need an army of experts to store the radioactive waste has safely as possible for thousands of years to come, without any hope of gaining further benefit. It started off with the idea of "clean" energy production, but we're not sure anymore: the technology waste as now put us in a precarious position. Similarly, information technology could turn out to be a self-made trap. IT and the World Wide Web have created enormous opportunities, but they also brought to an end our previously known and invaluable personal privacy. We cannot yet estimate the consequences, but it seems at a minimum to have succeeded in promoting more war and less democracy.

Wouldn't it be better to question how useful cars really are in general, for example, and to think about what alternatives we have to cars rather than stipulating their fuel efficiency? The car suggests that everybody has the ability to do what they want, and this fallacy obscures the view, because a network is needed in order to operate and make use of the cars. Even the name was a marketing trick right from the start: the car for everyone, the Volkswagen [German for "people's car"], was an invention of the Third Reich intended for economic growth, expansion, and warmongering.

Instead of thinking about how much energy we need to heat or cool our rooms, we should ask ourselves how many square meters of space we actually need. Today's construction means that much less energy is consumed in comparison to the 1960s, but the demand for space has risen sharply since then, and even goods were produced in the sixties in much smaller quantities at much less expense. Thus, it is not enough to establish laws regulating the CO_2 consumption per dwelling unit; it would also be necessary to limit the consumption per user.

Aren't the many "green building" concepts and populist sustainability slogans actually there much more for the sake of economic growth, which needs consumers like us as a base? Siren calls for "smart cities" and "smart living" delude about problems that are already known and clearly not yet solved, obscure the view, and create new deceptions. Gregor Gysi has rightly said: "For years, we have been demanding more affordable housing, more teachers, and better care. Now this is finally being discussed!" Gysi refers here to the discussions around the refugee debate and the accompanying absurdity that the poorest of all people are now reminding us of our wealth, and that it would have been necessary long ago to use that wealth sensibly and to redistribute it fairly. Electric cars, ecologically fair clothing, tomatoes free of genetic modifications, organic pharmaceutical products, non-toxic building materials, et cetera: who can afford that? Who would want to pay for that? What is the point of selling sustainability that way? Isn't this more of a hindrance to progress, and merely a further development of the status quo, designed to increase consumption? Can a society based on a growing economy even achieve true sustainability? As the engine of all change, burning criticism is required of everyone.

We are technologically equipped at the highest level possible: everyone has everything, and whenever possible it's always new. This is how individuals become prolific consumers and controllable citizens—we become cyborgs! Europe's future will then quite possibly look like what we know from dictatorships around the world: Those with enough money live apart from others, in fenced-in and guarded enclaves, someday maybe even on Mars. All communication takes place via controllable digital media. And when viewed in this light, what seems to be a place of togetherness is in truth isolation; real fellowship is hindered. Do we really want the technological shell to obstruct the way out?

What did Schiller and Beethoven mean in their Ode to Joy when they called out, "All men become brothers"? What does that mean given the fact that today we build fences and enlarge divides? Would the two today wish for "individual consumption" instead of "brotherhood"? Is it just a sentimental daydream—much like art is often misunderstood—and are we in fact mainly concerned with consolidating our economic, social, and cultural identity with the goal of living close to ourselves, for as long and as comfortably as possible? It appears that no one feels responsible for clearing the fog that obscures the negative effects of technology. Too great is the fear of giving up what has already been achieved and is familiar to us. Instead of continuing to serve economic growth by camouflaging our actions with ostensible sustainability, we must find a way to free ourselves from our cyborg mentality and seek instead active interaction between the elements. The solution is not transferable; it cannot be seen as God-given and the blame cannot be put on the political dreams of those in authority. Each of us must start with ourself. There must be early warning systems against the negative developments of existing terminologies. This must be part of our children's upbringing and education, so they can develop an awareness of what each individual can and must do to make a contribution. Instead of waiting for the outcomes of randomly controlled scientific research and their technological implementation, we must continually reinvent, elaborate, and defend the guardian function of independent and original thought!

So, I had imagined that now the questions will come—but there's nothing!

Without an awareness of the deeper tectonics of society's prevailing mood, we become "spectators" or "actors" instead of "architects," as Nietzsche put it. It should always be the other who intervenes. Are we too well equipped, too warmly dressed, too well-fed, such that our senses give us a feeling of security and in consequence a kind of rigidity sets in?

One's free choice of profession naturally brings with it a certain, more or less defined mission within any society based on the division of labor. It presumes that each individual who fulfills his or her responsibility can, in return, rely on securing a livelihood, even as a person under guardianship, sick and old. It is natural for a practicing physician to help other people, just as it is natural for a mother to support and nurture her children. We no longer have this direct challenge in other professions like judges, lawyers, civil servants, consultants, scientists, teachers, artists, or architects.

Thus, with the exception of mothers and physicians, we are all reliant on our local community to not harbor any ill intentions against us.

The division of labor leads to alienation and specialization, which ultimately means that we others have a vital interest in contributing to the positive development of the collective.

Upon recognizing that this machinery of our society no longer works along the periphery, our sensory apparatus ought to ensure that a practiced rebellion takes place.

Before we allow ourselves to be frightened by the tabloid press, populist slogans, and conservative explanations of the world, we should attempt to take the bull by the horns and overcome our own rigidity. Instead, we should see this as an opportunity for a new era and actively support especially those who are forced to leave their homes because the basic necessities for life are being cut off by external forces.

In this way, humaneness could take the place of politics and religion. A positive mood must be fostered: arrogance must be drawn into the glaring light and eradicated. The fight against terrorism, for example, can only be waged together with those who flee from it. Otherwise, we would have to resign together with Nietzsche when he says: "The fundamental belief is dying out, on the basis of which one could calculate, promise and anticipate the future in one's plan, and offer it as a sacrifice thereto, that in fact man has only value and significance in so far as he is a stone in a great building; for which purpose he has first of all to be solid, he has to be a 'stone.' ... Above all, not a-stage-player!"

We should build the most useful house, the most beautiful house—a house that serves as a symbol of our values! The golden cages with their long-gone and outmoded celebrity should be torn down and surrendered to ridicule! Georg Driendl

3

Spaceship

An ancient fairy tale tells of the construction of an ark, with which we will escape the approaching catastrophe. The capacity to bring along others is limited, however, so only a minimum number of each species, just enough to ensure procreation, is allowed on-board. Thus, the possibility of escape is linked from the beginning to a process of selection. Nonsense! Of course we won't accept that. We'll find something that enables us to take along everyone and everything. We'll find new spaces, new ships, new worlds, and this is exactly the dream we want to dream. A life like in a spaceship, a first look-out after birth, combined with a severe pain, and then unfortunate naivety as a child. Finished with school, confronted with the edifice of knowledge of the ancients, love saves us until the first disappointment ... We're all aboard this spaceship, heading on a collision course.

lonely at the end of the beginning
so it is unfulfilled and unliberated; sad, unimagined,
and lonely at the end of the beginning
days of the golden touch in the twilight will come again no more
it will not go, where to?

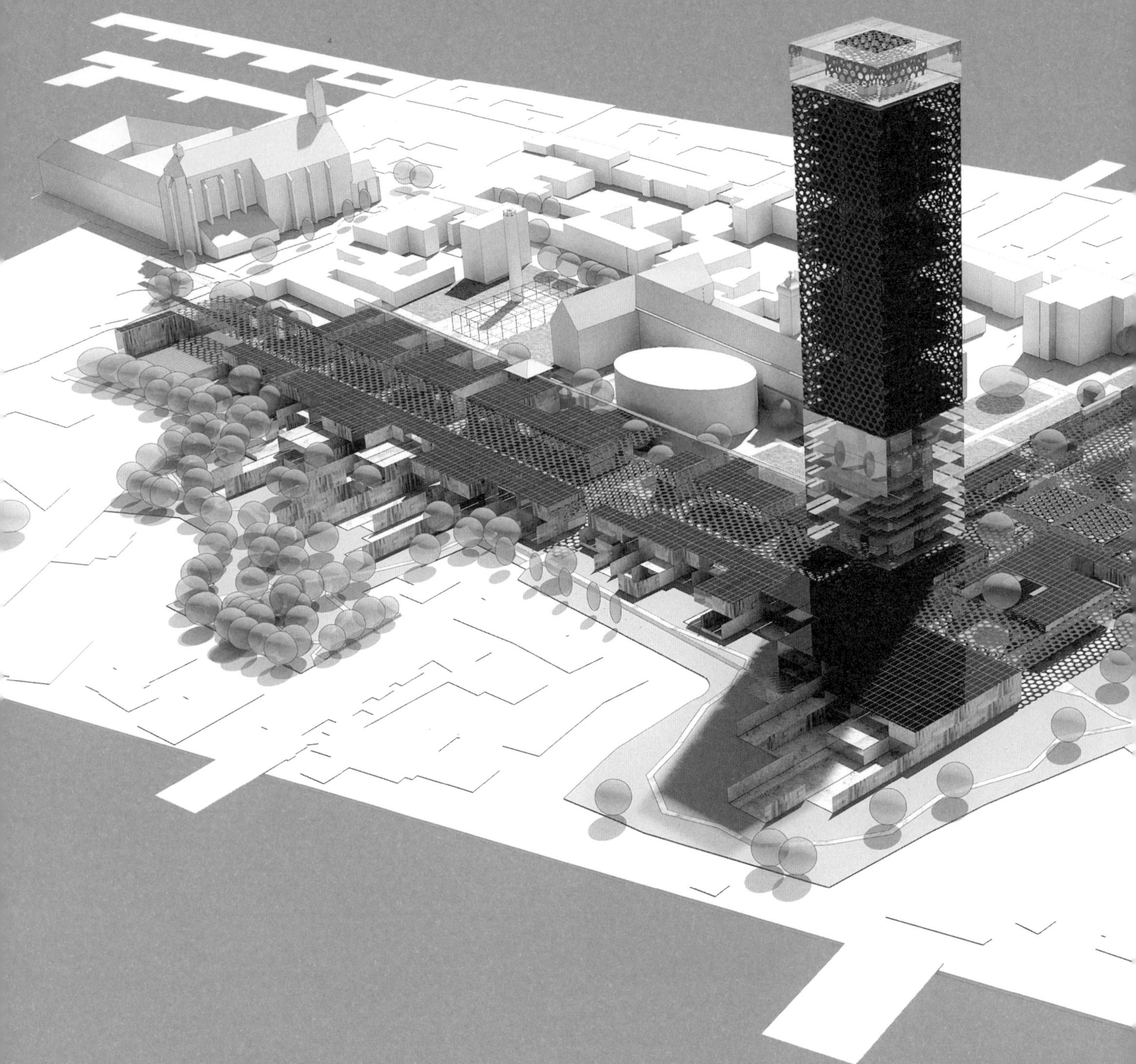

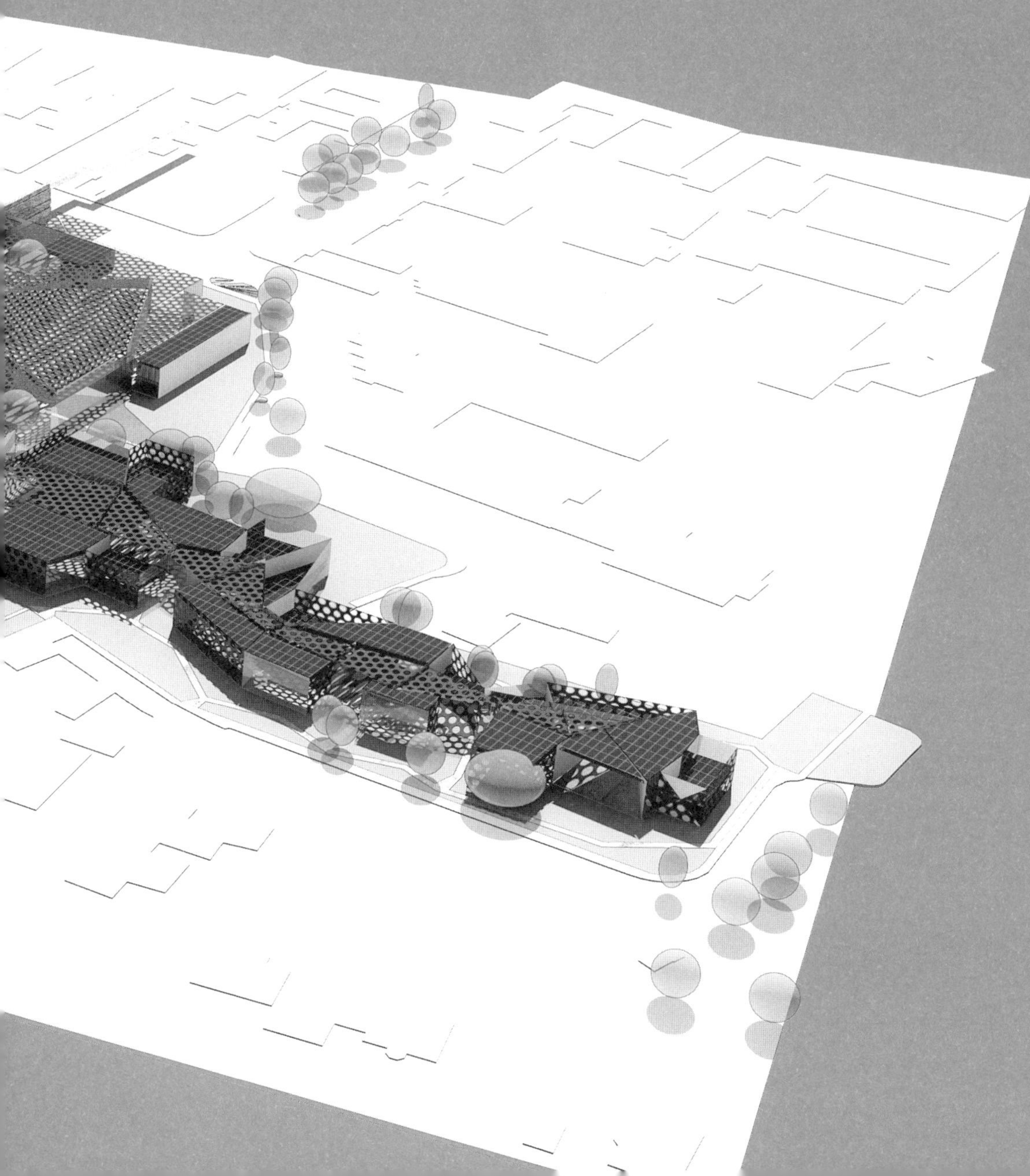

"… emitting less carbon is
not a substitute for emitting none"

The Economist

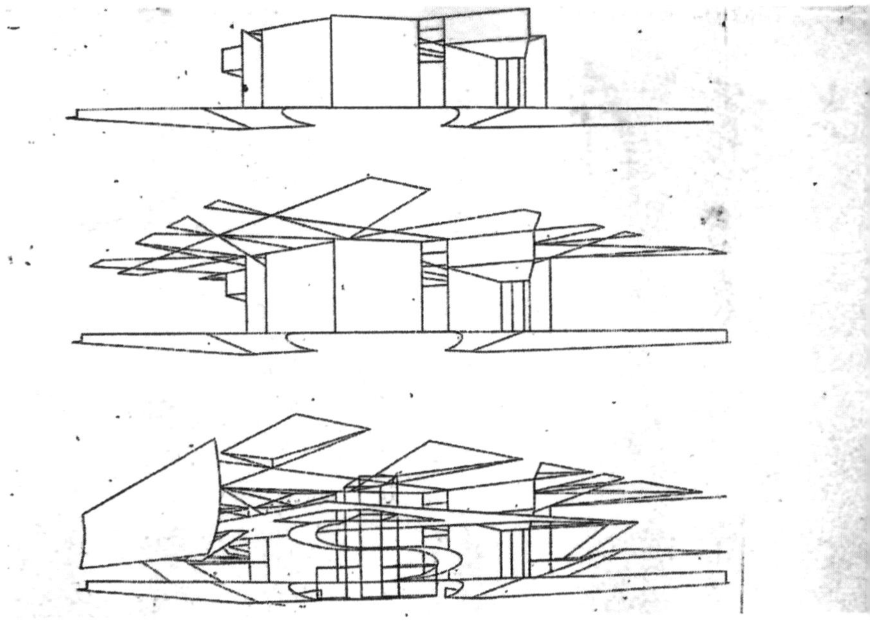

club

castle in the air
atmospheric air layer
balloonist giannozzo
airtight
airless

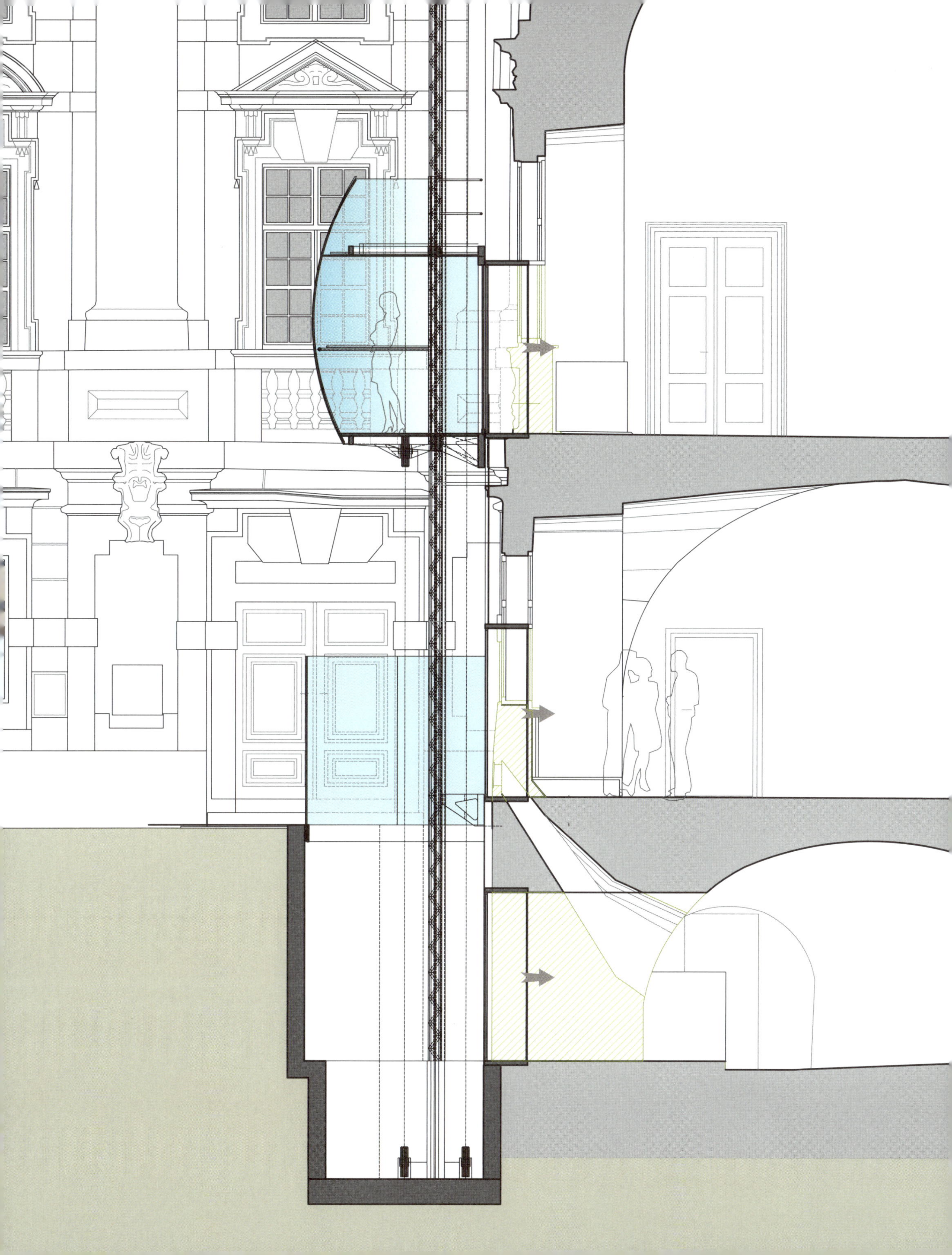

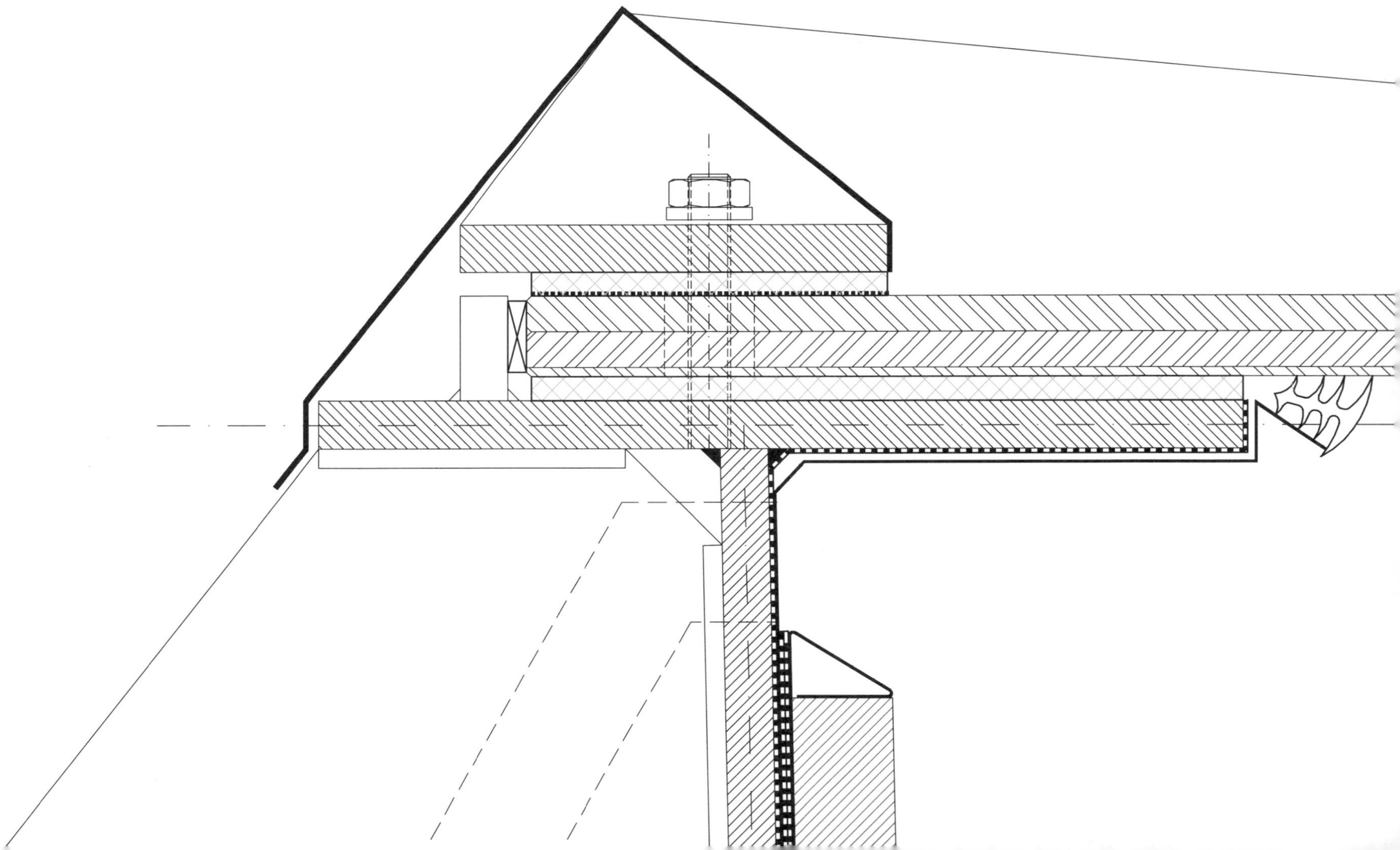

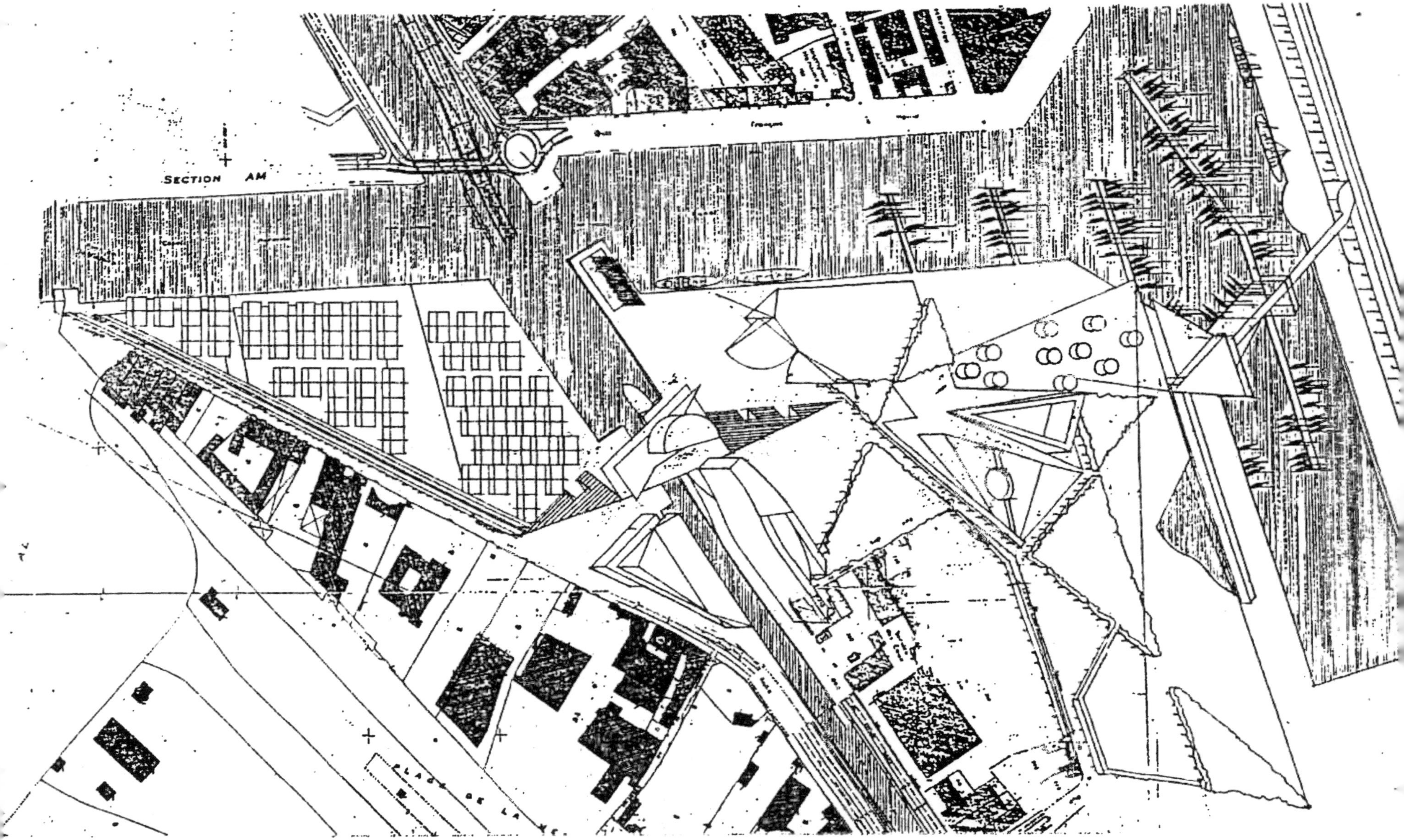
SECTION AM
PLACE DE LA

HAUS
RUDI MATT

water turns to mass
and hardens in the oncoming current
it flows no more because of the wall upstream

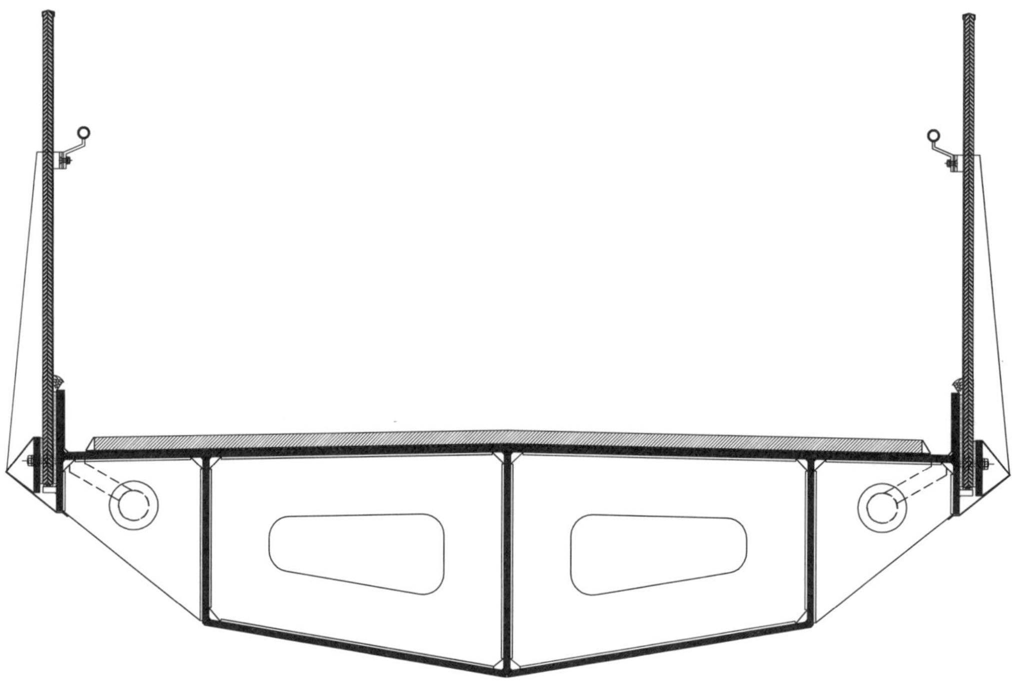

what's new

renewal?
newness?
new is what?
inexhaustible source?
ostentatious facade?
is that new?
optimization of the status quo
is not new
thus
in other words
what he doesn't know
is new
new
is
unknown

The Plan

There once was a time when rituals and symbols were derived from real events and passed down from generation to generation. The lives of individuals might end, but their knowledge and skills were continually handed down, producing artworks and buildings that far outlasted their creators. Many of our signs and customs come down to us through the built world since numerous buildings often survive over several generations, even civilizations. For this reason, I would now like to trace an arc back into the distant past and take a short walk through the history of architecture, only to return to the *modern age*, that is, the present.

If you imagine a thing from the distant past, something both mysterious and disconcerting, you will immediately think of the pyramids in Giza. They endure to this day as silent witnesses of a very distant, long-lost civilization that we can try to grasp scientifically or emotionally, but whose secrets remain intact. They were built according to a plan that is still perplexing, a slice of enigmatic, multi-layered space-time and cosmological references. The huge stone blocks were created with an almost unbelievable precision, even by today's standards, by workers using the simplest of technologies and most likely living under despotic rule. We may only guess the symbolism that corresponds with these built remnants of a bygone ruling culture, a culture organized and passed down in their day by ancient priests who carried its secrets to their graves. What survives is the sense of wonder, or fantasy even more so, as these buildings have remained almost completely intact, aside from some looting, over millennia. The mysterious pyramids: space-time buoys, variously reflecting almost every civilization that has followed, right up to today.

As the Renaissance established modern banking in Europe, it reactivated world trade and science. Cultural history was restored, one might even say *reinvented*. I quote from the foreword to Leon Battista Alberti's *Ten Books on Architecture* in which Angelus Politianus addresses Lorenzo de' Medici: "I would like you, Lorenzo, to give this book a place of honor in your library, read it carefully yourself, and make sure that it is widely published. For it is worthy to live on the lips of the learned, and the patronage of the arts, abandoned by all others, rests with you alone. Farewell." Alberti's *Ten Books* were based mainly on the 15th century writings of Vitruvius, and they examined from a fresh perspective the entire field of construction: the sources, quality and usability of materials, and everything from construction techniques, typologies and the founding of cities to infrastructure and transport, machinery and warfare. On the subject of Egypt's building culture, Alberti writes: "But no nation was more diligent than were the Egyptians with their sepulchers: they maintained that men were wrong to make the house unduly sumptuous—being their residence for so brief a time—at the expense of the sepulcher, which would be their place of rest for so long."

Our next highlights representing an all-but-forgotten building culture shining up to us from the dim past (though a bit closer in time) come from the Ancient Greeks, in particular the Parthenon atop the Acropolis in Athens. The surviving writings of the Greeks serve as testimonies that help bring their architectural remains into focus. The Parthenon was built in the 5th century BC under the direction of Athen's ruler Pericles. Today it is a sad sight, not due to the ravages of time but rather senseless warfare that caused its half-ruined state. Once again, this building—a temple—was constructed from individual pieces of precisely matched stone. The joinery is such that, despite an almost unbelievable mathematical and geometric complexity, the temple's base has a slight upward curve, each column was given *entasis* and the columns lean slightly inward. The stonework is so exact that cracks caused by earthquakes traverse from one section to the next as if they were a seamless monolith rather than individual building blocks, each unlike any other. Recently, marble sections of one column were separated for research purposes, and it was reported that one could still smell the wooden connectors that had been incorporated to aid in assembly 2500 years before. The whole structure is, for us, a *gesamtkunstwerk* of ideal beauty, and one completed within a short construction time. Once again, we today lack the kind of comprehensible plan from which the politically democratic Athens drew its genius. More from the Renaissance Alberti: "... and they did not fail to examine every single part, even the most insignificant thing: how right fits to left, the upright to the horizontal, the near to the most distant. They connected and separated, compared larger with smaller, similar with dissimilar, the first with the last until it was perfectly clear that one must praise certain aspects of a structure built for eternity and others in those built for smaller purposes, such as pleasure. So it was with this one." The Greeks, as a nation of artists and philosophers, assumed that the state belonged to its citizens. They were the first to recognize that the legal institution of private property was a necessity, and that, in emergencies, the state should provide for its citizens, either through public funds or at the expense of its wealthier citizens. Tenants and landlords, lessors and lessees shared approximately the same legal status.

On the other hand, the power-conscious Romans needed a more forceful legal system from the start in order to expand their empire. They made a sharp distinction between property and possessions, putting the property owner in a much stronger legal position than the tenant or lessee. Stylistically, the Romans adopted characteristics of Greek architecture but further developed and enhanced all their building types.

The Coliseum and the Pantheon represent completely new building types created by the Romans and still copied to this day. The Pantheon, for example, was built using an unprecedented hybrid construction: a rotunda with a cast-concrete dome whose inscribed sphere measures 43 meters in diameter. The essential difference between Roman and Greek building cultures came through the production of a prefabricated part, bricks made of fired clay, and the resulting development of the arch, the barrel vault and the pendentive. One famous and impressive example is the Baths of Caracalla complex in Rome which remains today as a ruin. Here, too, the damage was not the result of time but rather destruction and looting resulting from the building being appropriated for alternate functions.

Within a short time, the Romans also had to create infrastructure for the lands they had conquered through military campaigns: build roads, install irrigation, erect defenses and appoint governors for the ever-expanding Roman Empire. But it is the aqueducts stretching across the whole empire that remain widely visible today as their crowning set pieces. The brick was a standardized building element that could, employing appropriate techniques, be shaped into nearly any form, produced anywhere and quickly installed—and thus fit this enormous building task perfectly. In the realm itself, the imperial plan seems to have been lost over time. "There is nothing that distinguishes one man from another more than this one point; in which he differs widely from the animals, in reason and understanding of the fine arts; or further, if you wish, in the prospering of his worldly goods." (Alberti) The Roman Empire was literally collapsing in on itself. Nobody wanted to carry on with their achievements except for: "... only the legal system, upon which an economically, technologically, financially and socially-backward Empire had failed in the distant past, was adopted by victorious capitalism as its functional basis. Its corruption into a modern slave economy was thus predetermined." (Wilhelm Hankel)

In Europe, there followed a dark period when conditions were re-established and reorganized. Architecturally, we have the rise of the Romanesque style, followed by Gothic. It was a time of curious centering on religious content, along with the expansion of religious power which culminated in buildings such as the cathedrals in Chartres and Reims, both pinnacles of superb stonemasonry. Here we find craftsmanship and adventurous engineering feats: Flying buttresses and ribbed vaults employ knowledge of static physics to delicately stiffen and transfer loads. The stained-glass rosette windows combined with the vaulting and arches engendered an almost symphonic spatial experience for the average man living nearby in a hygienically desolate shanty. Raids were waged in the name of the Cross and witches were burned, while pestilence dealt with the remainder of the oppressed and abused people. In the building sheds, the essential secret—the knowledge of architecture—was guarded, and its disclosure to outsiders was forbidden. It was as though the anonymous builders and craftsmen had been seized by a miraculous divine plan, one that vanished into darkness as suddenly as it had appeared. Then Alberti's voice rises out of the Renaissance, recalling the ancients, reorienting toward the future and away from anonymity: "Him I consider the architect, who by sure and wonderful reason and method, knows both how to devise through his own mind and energy, and to realize by construction, whatever can be most beautifully fitted out for the noble needs of man, by the movement of weights and the joining and massing of bodies. To do this he must have an understanding and knowledge of all the highest and most noble disciplines." And further: "Some have said that it was fire and water which were initially responsible for bringing men together into communities, but we, considering how useful, even indispensable, a roof and walls are for men, are convinced that it was they that drew and kept men together. We are indebted to the architect not only for providing that safe and welcome refuge from the heat of the sun and the frosts of winter (that of itself is no small benefit), but also for his many other innovations, useful to both individuals and the public, which time and time again have so happily satisfied daily needs." (Alberti) The beginnings of building culture are clearly and bluntly defined: "Since this is the case, the elements of which the whole matter of building is composed are clearly six: locality, area, compartition, wall, roof, and opening ... If we were to consider those attributes with which each of the parts we have enumerated should be endowed, we would come up with three that should never be overlooked, and which are most becoming to roofs, openings, and so on. That is, their individual parts should be well suited to the task for which they were designed and, above all, should be very commodious; as regards strength and endurance, they should be sound, firm, and quite permanent; yet in terms of grace and elegance, they should be groomed, ordered, garlanded, as it were, in their every part." (Alberti) Finally, the verdict: "first we observe that the building is a kind of body consisting, like all other bodies, of matter and of *lineamenti*, the one the product of nature and the other the product of *ingenio*. The one dependent on preparation and selection and the other one arising from the mind and cognition. We realized, nevertheless, that without the hand of the skilled workman neither would suffice to fashion matter." (Alberti) A new age had arrived. Before, during and after Alberti's lifetime came singular, brilliant artists and architects such as Filippo Brunelleschi, Donato Bramante, Leonardo da Vinci, Michelangelo Buonarroti, Albrecht Durer, Raphael Sanzio da Urbino and Andrea Palladio. Palladio oversaw the veritable mass production of villas as a lead contractor working for wealthy Venetians. In 1580 he built the Teatro Olimpico on behalf of the Academy of Vicenza. Though Palladio did not live to see its completion, he had set out a three-dimensional monument to the idea of the Renaissance: the perspective view, projecting an eye's vision from a particular standpoint.

Originally funded and supported by individual families in feudal Italy, Renaissance art quickly spread throughout Europe thanks to the new art of printing. One critical voice from this period: "... in a place where all value is measured based on the standard of money, it will hardly be possible to pursue just and happy politics ..." writes Thomas More in his socio-political satire *Utopia*.

Out of feudalism and the principalities emerged a new absolutism whose splendor and glory, embodied in Baroque's illusion of heaven on earth, became exemplary of courtly life in the world of that time. The summit was reached with the Sun King Louis XIV and his palace at Versailles, constructed in the middle of France. In Austria, the Augustine Choirmasters planned their monastery in Klosterneuburg as a magnificent showplace according to the pious plans of the Holy Roman Emperor Charles VI, equal in size to the largest late-Renaissance building in the world, El Escorial. However, the trowels were dropped promptly upon Charles' death in 1740. What remained was an unfinished torso, and today you can still visit a Baroque construction site that was shut down in the middle of work.

Absolutism continued in Europe after the American and French Revolutions up to World War I despite the Enlightenment and compulsory education. Architecture was superficially characterized by classical and imperial-style façades, with corresponding historical references both in America and in Europe. One example of this is Vienna's Ring Road.

All dictatorships, even contemporary ones, use a specific language of form for public buildings to demonstrate power and to use the state as an instrument to consolidate unequal conditions. We can discern a very tenacious and slow awakening from the sleep of mystification.

The lofty democratic plan of the modern age, the liberation from everything handed down from history, as triggered by industrialization as well as democratic and social experimentation, was only able to assert itself slowly when confronted by the lumbering tank of dusty classics.

The transition to new tools began a rapid revolution in science and technology and led to a sense of almost boundless horizons. From the printing press came mass production, transportation and telecommunications. The suggestion of unlimited do-ability grows into a substitute for religion and politics. On January 4, 1922, Russian "biocosmists" printed their demand in the Moscow government newspaper *Izvestia* that, without delay, only two fundamental human rights should be recognized, namely the "right of being" and the "right of mobility in the cosmic space." It was no longer bearable to accept the "limitedness of man in time and space," even sanctioning it as a "natural necessity." Instead, they demanded, "... unlimited life and unhindered movement for all—even for the already deceased."! It took a new world war to raise the local storms of political *-isms* to the level of transcontinental resource security. "A state with sovereign citizens, with a truly independent judiciary and functioning separation of powers will not be weaker, but rather more legitimized through a stronger democracy. Anyone who has hitherto demanded a weaker state (especially in the USA) always asserted that we must surrender effective power to the market, that is, to the corporations and banks. In a modern democracy, alternatively, the task must be more to expose the workings of power to the will of its citizens whereby the highest good of law-making is found at the poles of liberty and equality, so difficult to reconcile." (Daniela Dahn) Global corporations dominate the instruments of opinion formation, food production, energy distribution, etc., while inspiring the fantasy that the individual can participate in a substantive way. Media, communications, aerospace and publishing are supplemented by the ubiquitous Internet. Robert Reich, the former Secretary of Labor under American President Bill Clinton, is convinced that, as it currently exists, democracy "is run by a few big interests looking out for themselves." Our interests as consumers and investors are well served, "but the citizen in us has almost vanished from politics." He calls for reforms to mobilize the public to enact legislative changes. "The decisive political conflict in the political party system," Hannah Arendt noted already in the 1960s, "is not between right and left, as everyone believes, but between the parliament and the people who have lost their power to their representatives."

The building planned by Apple for its new corporate headquarters in Cupertino, California brings us back to the theme of symbolism and building: a gigantic, multistoried, flat, homogeneous, circular ring on otherwise largely undeveloped land, an endless closed system from the pedestrian's perspective. A sign of everything and a program for eternity. We carry our trowel in our bag and toil as journeymen laborers perhaps in this moment, everything for some greater whole but not knowing the master plan. We no longer work on real buildings but on symbolic buildings, on the temple of humanity, on a humane society—that is, in theory, the plan. Georg Driendl

4

Coverlet

Suit, spacesuit, housecoat, street clothes, gala—clothes make the man—ermine, slim fit. The actor must be complaisant, provoke evocatively, and put on a good show. Clever camouflage allows the substance to be shifted to the back while something else entirely is then conveyed unabashedly in the foreground. The actor is torn between an intentionally employed pompous affectation and a sober "less is more" posturing; stuck in our overflowing universe of images, with no safe harbor, we are driven by the search to catch a glimpse behind the scenes that restrict our horizon, and, at least for a brief moment, to be a witness of what is. Beneath the coverlet slumbers the uncanny power to manifest illusions and to deduce wrong conclusions therefrom.

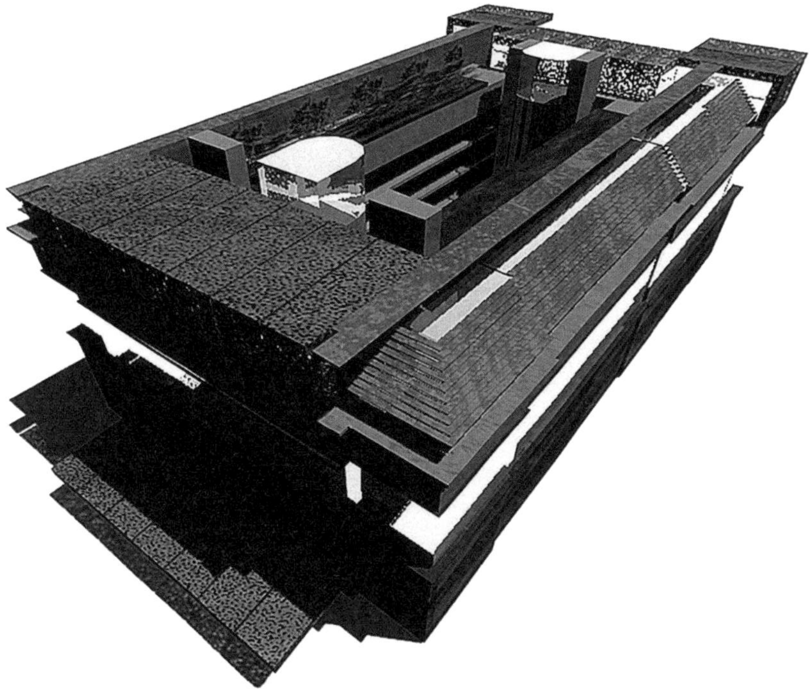

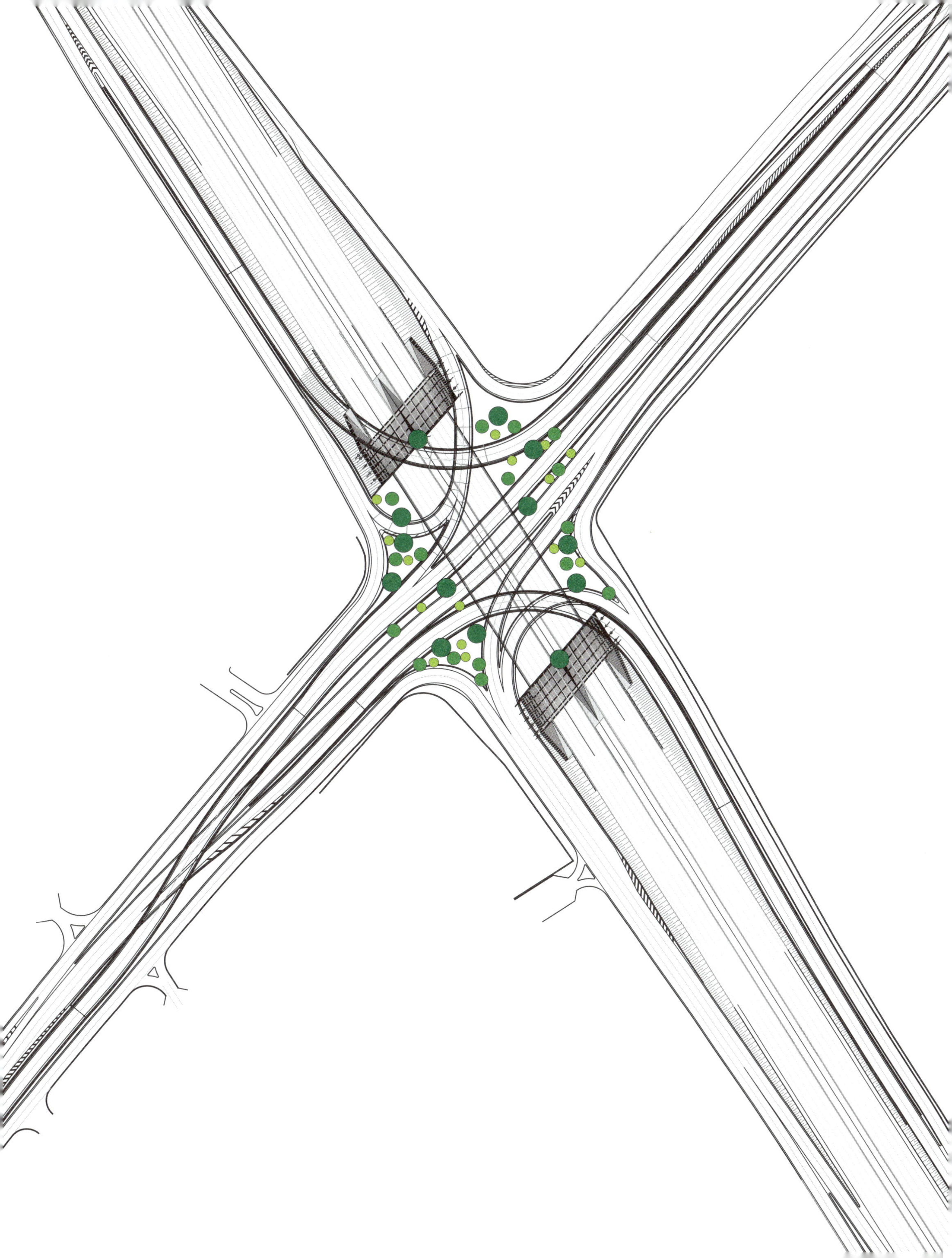

sett-eyed
bue-eyed
blue-eyed
wide-eyed
beautifully eyed
big-eyed
eyed
oi

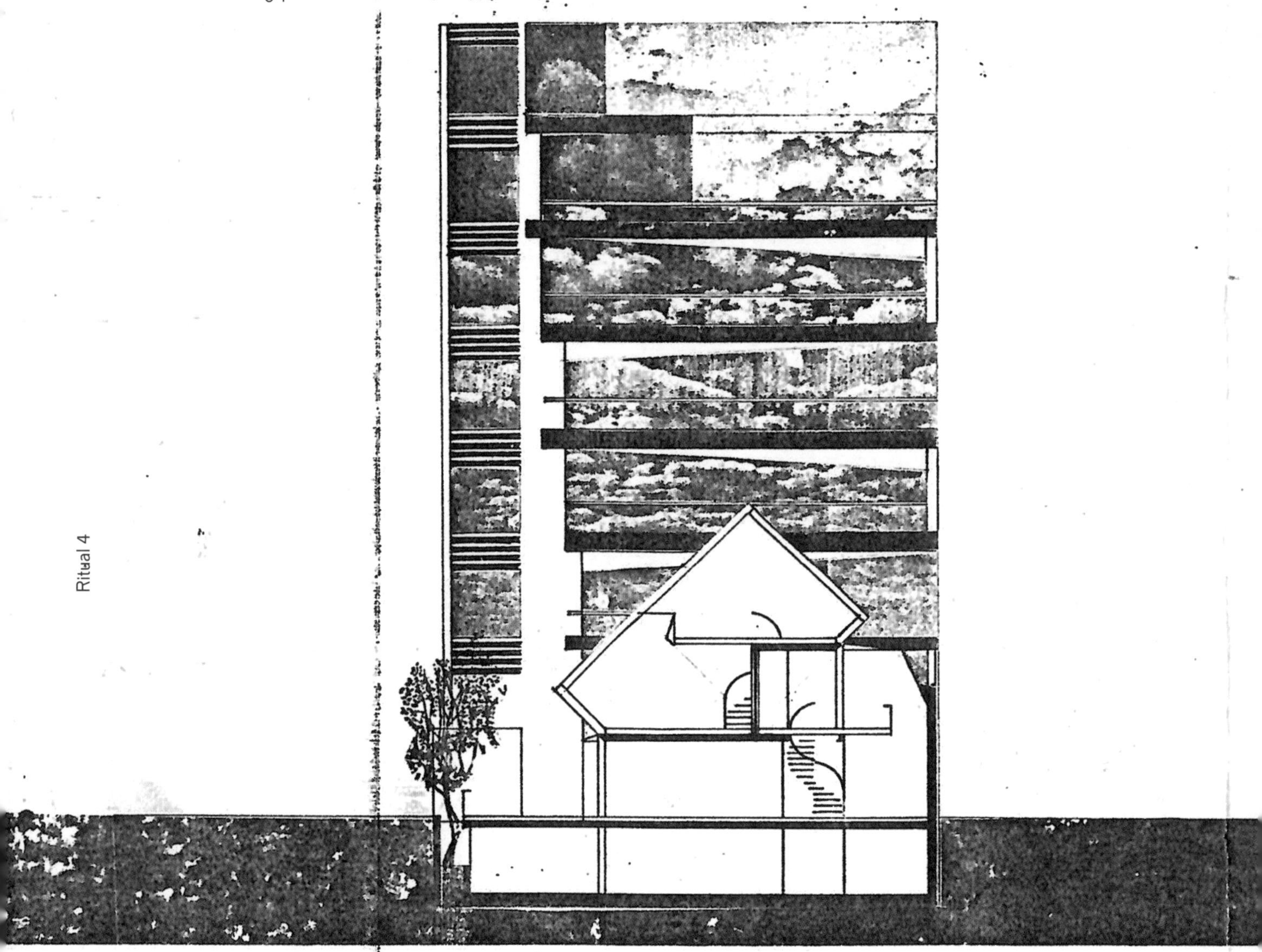

Schnittansicht Hof 1:200

TT5 Twist Tower five

Dunkle Zeiten
Blick zurück
Leopold III.
Leopold III

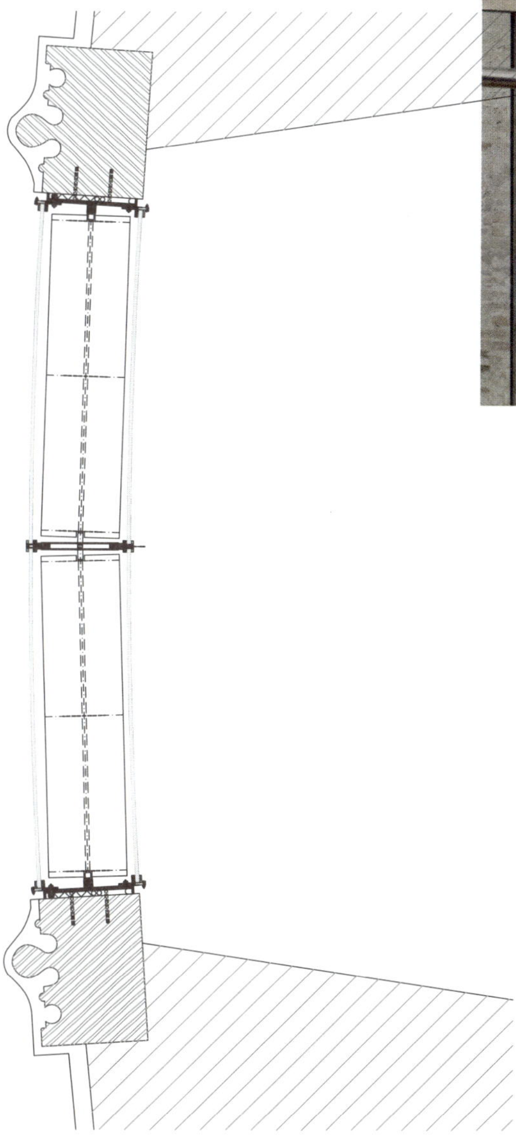

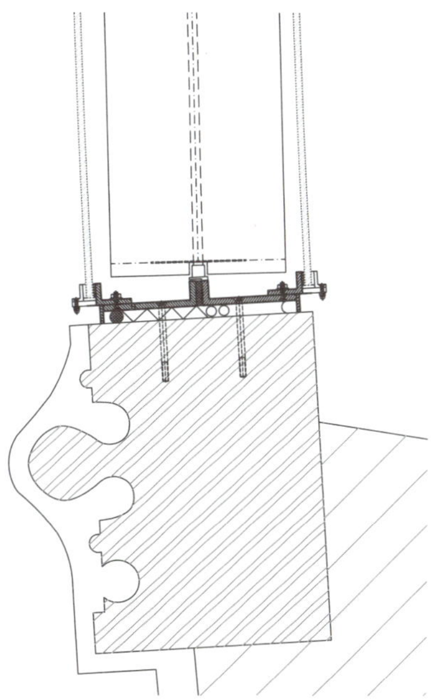

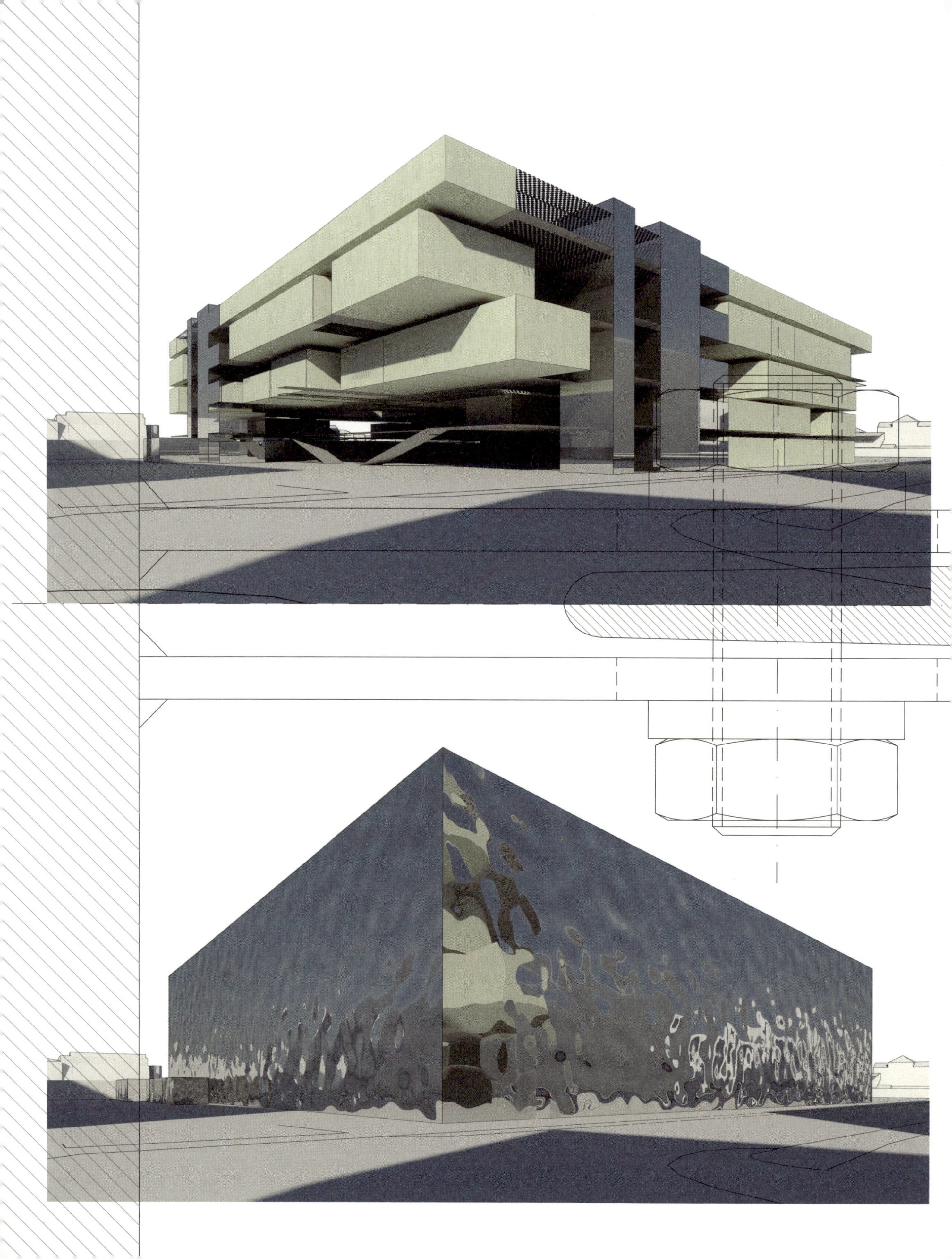

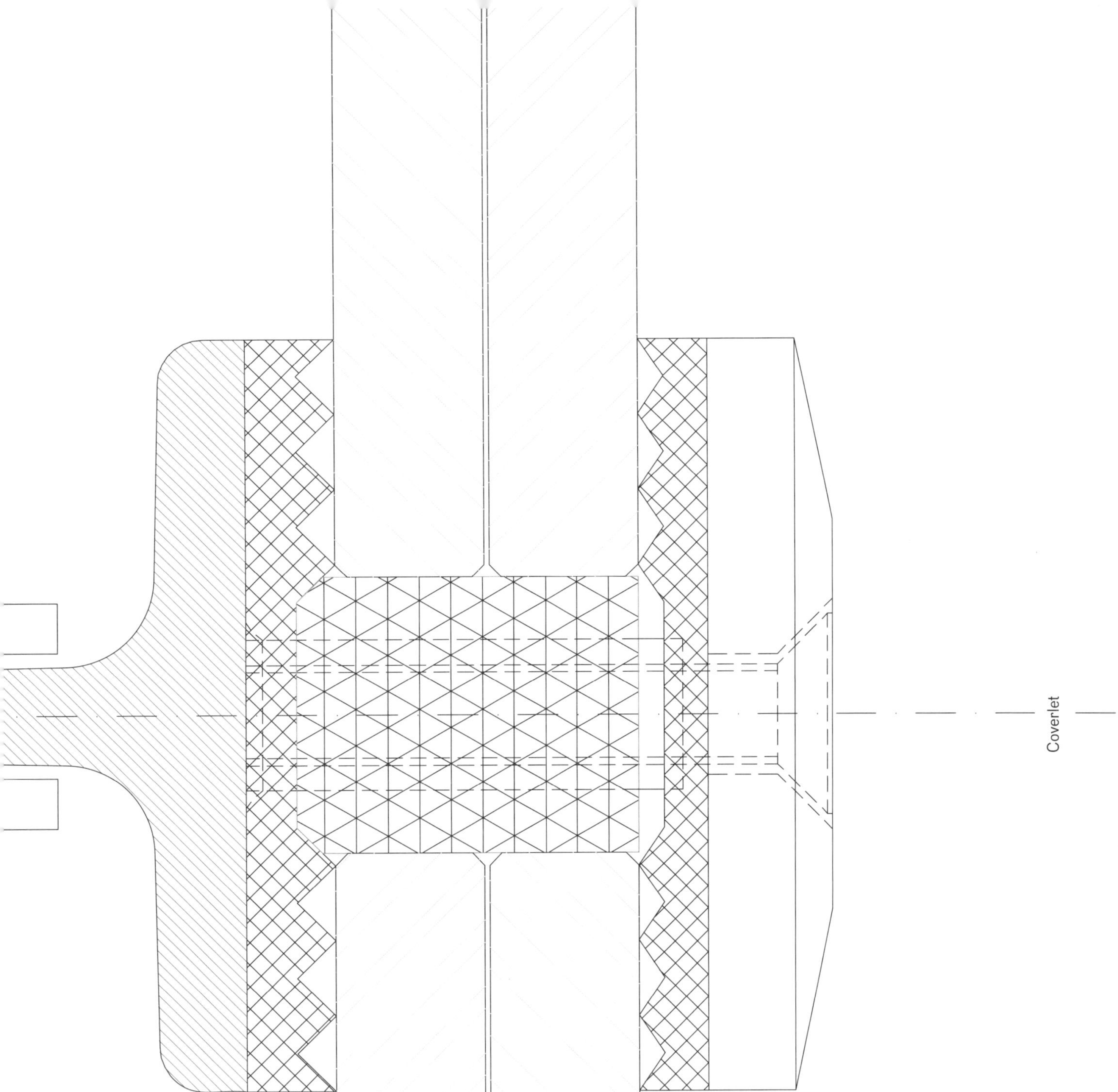

When asked about beauty, Einstein responded:
"In the interest of clarity, I have found it unavoidable to repeat myself often, without paying any regard whatsoever to the elegance of presentation; from the scientific point of view, I have conscientiously adhered to the precept of the brilliant theoretician L. Boltzmann, that one should let elegance be a matter for the tailors and shoemakers."

air
airtight
build airtight
build tightly
build

even very small, infinitely small, one does not really fit in, it's tight and cramped on all sides, it pokes and stabs and yet sometimes on side a light, over there is something different … oh, smile

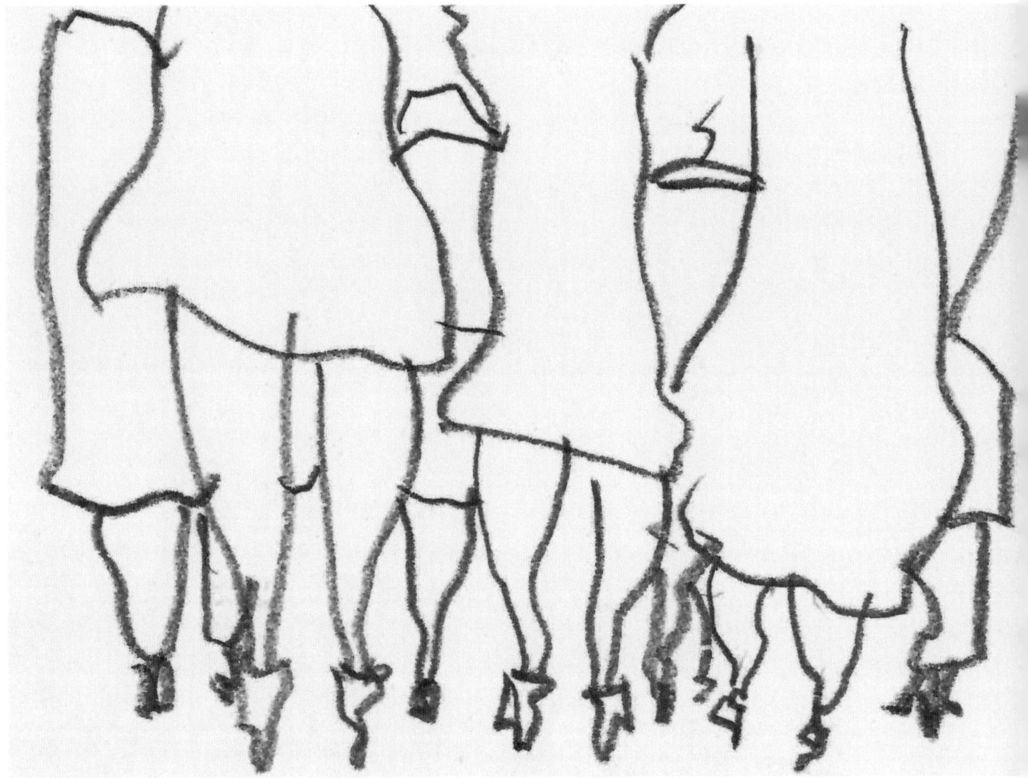

house
casing
house
housing
question of housing
in the case
weightless
timeless
irrespective of the weather
flash-frozen
secure from eavesdropping
germ-free
insulated
through the air

The Beauty of Work

The right to work is a fundamental right, and beauty is an ideal. We work, and beauty adds the finishing touch. Our sensual selves hope that the work we do is beautiful in the end.

Obtaining a view of the meaning of this relationship—airy, light, quasi in a flyby—that was the idea.

However, I soon had to recognize that this topic is highly charged and that merely clearing away the associated and often inappropriate use would not suffice. Nevertheless, driven by the courage to accept a healthy naivety, what first and foremost occurred to me is that any work, especially with one another, is beautiful, can be beautiful, or even better, should be beautiful, and more than that, that the products of work ought to engender beauty—but it's just not that simple.

If you google "work," you come across Karl Marx and various organizations that claim work for themselves in a variety of ways. And if you google "beauty," you get models. On the face of it, work is a political category and beauty is an ideal or a desired image.

In the philosophical sense, "work" is understood as the willful creative action of people. This action is employed for a variety of political and religious goals, as a social engine, and for the production of the respective desired conditions as workers. The resulting outcomes—such as temples, palaces, cathedrals, social insurance, agriculture, mobility, strawberries and grapes in the winter, or long-distance travels as status symbols—make working people aware of the guiding idea while simultaneously moving the ideal far out of reach.

"Beauty" is derived from the "splendor of truth" (veritatis splendor) and Kant's "disinterested enjoyment." In our encyclopedia we find: "... embellishes and decorates the building [...]. Tolerance, the willingness to help, charity, and brotherly love are expressions of true beauty."

In modern times, the term is then critically challenged, and a decorative work that is merely beautiful is deemed "kitsch." But on the contrary, beauty—even if not primarily in art—arises almost by itself. When we spend our time in nature, for instance, our feeling is that life is beautiful.

Life itself does not differentiate between nature and art: "The living is that which has an interest in itself, which is concerned about itself, and reacts accordingly," says Andreas Weber, biologist and philosopher.

Basically, we have to realize that beauty can only ever be relative; it cannot be absolute, even though this expectation is expressed time and again. The very question of which man is the most handsome would lead to a highly surprising result for men—especially if women are the ones being asked. In our lives together, in our relationships and in society, we recognize beauty in the knowledge that this precious objective requires much work on one's own self. We see all the more critically from a personal perspective that beauty as a whole will not succeed in absolute terms.

In ordinary life, I am constantly confronted with demonstrating, depicting, or even manifesting beauty as the result of a work process, and to do so in its entirety. That means: cheap, sustainable, fit for use, standardized, lawful, and so on. The list gets longer as more people are involved only passively, as observant guardians of the identical, forced into the work process. The role of defense becomes part of everyday life.

Today's equivalents of the Bauhütte—this is a bit of a stretch—exist less in Europe and more in Asia, Africa, and the Middle East—where that which we take for granted and which may have already become useless has not yet been built: cities, airports, power plants, factories, traffic routes, and other infrastructural facilities.

In a real Bauhütte in a container village in the middle of the desert, I have the honor of directing a symbol of creative work in opposition to nature and for the sake of beauty. Here, in constant dialogue with the client, Muzahim—an Arab who is always on site and has an eye for everything—people of all kinds work on a common endeavor: from the "Irishman," head of the laboratory and a brilliant chemist, to the pipe-smoking, contract-forging Englishman, the Austrian road designer, the Australian project manager Peter, the Egyptian theoretician and businessman, and the masterful Polish engineer—he is simply known as "the Pole"—to the Spanish quality inspector Luis, the Dutch garden planner Ed, the rigorous German graphic artist who overlooks nothing, and the construction firms, led by a Lebanese general contractor with his staff of experts. The list goes on. Every interdisciplinary discussion takes place only in the presence of Muzahim. As soon as he becomes aware of a dialogue among more than two parties, without delay he convenes a meeting in the big conference room with everyone involved. Of course much is said, including unproductive attempts at thwarting agreement, but the swift public attention to the matters in question means that any quarrel and each foreign element is immediately taken up and resolved.

That was completely new for me: as the driving force, the client himself wants to solve the problems down to the last detail, face to face. Three young employees, also Arabs, support him in these efforts. Those men are in turn supported by Filipinos, who are responsible for all the clerical work and the finances—led by Sunny. Every now and then, someone with a new idea comes onto the site and the chatter immediately spreads like wildfire—Who is that? What does he want? That ceases when he speaks with the big boss, Muzahim. Does he have something to offer or not? That's it.

Here, there is no preconceived plan that is simply implemented; it is instead created in an almost entirely natural way—through an exciting field of unconventional procedural problem solving. One could wax literarily sentimental and say: This harsh climate shapes or congeals the matter into a single option. This city is creating itself, no one knows where the journey is going; the plan is the goal, but the plan undergoes constant change, like the dunes in the desert.

What if the Arab, as the eternal son of the desert, simply has the better idea about life in the desert, but nevertheless has the greatness to seek advice from the green region? He builds the city with our imagination, but it comes alive through his.

Process

We can observe that, in the pursuit of self-enrichment, entire occupational groups disguise their collective intelligence as highly complex work. I have the right to make this blanket criticism of the conventional export of services, in full knowledge that a great many positive things are also being done. A dispute, for example, is not regarded there as a dynamic factor of a development and viewed positively, but simply exaggerated utterly senselessly and often downright destructively. In the Bauhütte in the desert, this takes care of itself, and one focuses on the iterative process under the auspices of direct accountability.

The parallel world to work is consumption. Should individual consumer behavior ultimately lead to the well-being of all? That is in any case what the high doctrine of economics wants us to believe. Is it the goal of a thoroughly rationalized, efficient, economically oriented society based on the division of labor to carry things so far that everyone must work hard beyond their limits so that a few can live a good life? Perhaps the situation could be inverted, proclaiming beauty as a political goal and work as an ideal. In this round dance, art is given the task of awakening an archaic basic sense, so as not to lose meaning in a complex, work-sharing process.

Paradise

In the beginning, Adam and Eve were in paradise. It was beautiful, but they were without work. Paradise is considered the epitome of primal beauty: everything is in harmony, everything is natural, there is no influence from humans, there is no one there who consciously works creatively to disturb or change nature. Everything is at rest. Without work, a person has beautiful and of course also ugly thoughts.

This story lives on today in multifunctional irony, as in Cockaigne, the mythical land of plenty, where indulgence is considered a virtue and work is a sin, and where a fountain bestows eternal youth: "He who has an old woman / he takes her with him to the watering place / they bathe barely three days / a young lass will you have / of about eighteen years old." [freely translated from a 17th century German ballad]

Nature

In its "proto-beauty," nature awakens our taste for work, endlessly provoking us to action. There must be something here that can be changed to better fit our ideas. As a refuge, we devise the notion of the "beautiful" in addition to the "primal beauty" of nature. Even on the walls of early caves, nature was abstracted and created anew, perhaps to banish ugliness and to reflect the nature within us. Technology and the shared process of the conscious will to work (with the appropriate ritual) is born, and thus art emerges alongside nature—that is, alongside the "primal beauty" of nature, the beauty created by humans as a manifestation of our will.

On the 11th tablet of the Epic of Gilgamesh, the ferryman Urshanabi tells Gilgamesh the story of Ziusudra, who, warned by God, builds a boat and escapes the flood disaster with his entire kin and all the animals of the steppe. In the course of his search for immortality, Gilgamesh finds the plant of eternal youth, which, however, is stolen from him by a snake.

The biblical Noah goes much further: He consciously sets himself to work and builds the ark. The idea of choosing to flee from nature begins here; the wheel begins to spin, unstoppably, and the journey into the future becomes longer and longer.

When driving past, we realize that nature is in fact beautiful, although sometimes inhospitable and only usable under certain conditions. Hence: Get to work, brimming with a zest for action; onward, onward! What stands still withers. Movement becomes the goal.

Fresh Start

Civilization is shaped by work and beauty as a dynamic model opposed to nature. The laws pertaining to orderly cultivation, whose condensed abstractions are perceived by us as beautiful and which were discovered over the course of time through specialized scientific work, are the basis and the driving force of progress.

The mostly dramatic process of design and creation constitutes work that pushes the limits of resilience and whose outcome is uncertain. Plagued by self-doubt as to whether a solution can ever be found, an extremely tense mental state ensues, between wistful anticipation and the most severe depression stemming from the flash of inspiration that refuses to strike. We become restless, forget our neighbors, hope for something out of the ordinary, see in everything and everyone a disruption of progress, and have the feeling of being put on the spot. As in a dream, the otherwise so confident demeanor is distorted and decelerated in what are actually familiar surroundings; we had thought that everything was okay. Moreover, stipulations—that are usually defined retroactively by a politically motivated management, economically drilled to seek profits and pursue technocratic objectives that border on the absurd—are specified and enforced. Once that process has begun, well-founded reasoning that speaks against a particular objective, or perhaps for a change of course or the need for new thinking, no longer matters at all. That which has been set into motion is unthinkingly followed through, whatever the cost, while stocks last, rightly or wrongly, and if necessary it vanishes from the scene. There is no one personally behind the execution. Everything is arbitrary, and as slippery as an eel.

But if, amid the conflicting priorities, the intensive work on the matter unexpectedly yields a spontaneous idea that presents a very simple solution for everything, that is the tranquil moment of beauty in our work—and all the employed forces are suddenly in cosmic balance. The ensuing, mostly irrational conclusion that something has thereby changed drives us to the next uncertain threshold. That is the movement of progress, not the individual outcomes of the process in which we allow ourselves to become entangled. Hence our view of the essential tends to be clouded; we experience and exist while driving past.

Technology

The technology we develop in this way will never be finished or perfect for the purposes of our ever-growing ambitions. On the contrary, a gradual feeling of powerlessness arises with regard to the insidious everyday process of technological encroachment into all spheres of life. Even wishful thinking is projected onto the technology, and applicable solutions are already being offered in the pre-future. The Ossi had to wait for the Trabi, but the iWatch came before anyone even thought of needing it. On our very wrists, we now experience an informational paradise of everything we want to know. In this new paradise, sensuous contact with nature is replaced by information. The result is the battle of "each against the other," armed with the technology we all developed collectively, probably in the wake of the old-fashioned wars over religion and resources, a new and unavoidable challenge.

Some mysteries of our forgotten past remind us in exemplary manner that work undertaken in a collective effort with regard to the ideal of beauty has congealed into a work of art. The tools we have developed are indeed employed, but they are no guarantee that a soul resides within the resulting products.

The question of whether the Venus of Willendorf is a fertility symbol or represents an ideal of beauty will likely never be answered conclusively. Whether symbol or ideal, in either case it is interesting to note that, despite exhibiting great detail, no face is depicted or even suggested. And what does Nefertiti tell us, that face with peculiar make-up and odd headdress from beyond the grave of history, which, in its contemporary presentation within a museum context, appears to have been suddenly taken from life? Art and its underlying work process are capable of transporting an ideal of beauty over millennia, transcending both space and time. "There are women who are not beautiful but only look that way," Karl Kraus would have said.

Surgery

In both mathematics and architecture, beauty is directly linked to simplicity, and often even equated with it. The mathematical constant *pi* has been known since antiquity and can now be calculated to a bazillion decimal places, yet it is never finished, never final, and nonetheless always correct. The circle remains a circle and is an approximate idea, hence it cannot be squared. But we live in the dimension of quadrature, of squaring the circle—and not triangulation nor any other sphere, even though something else would be theoretically possible.

When, to put it simply, content and form coincide, when fundamental laws reveal themselves in an easy-to-understand way in relation to our existence, the city as the antithesis to nature, and also the human construct known as the theory of everything, what then ...? Of course architecture had to burn in 1968, and now it is being corrected; it had to burn in our minds—that was true back then, and so we are told today!

Mathematics is in this regard more stable, and less fashionable, because beautiful formulas are valid until they are refuted.

Wrangling also goes on in music—especially new music, where beauty is practically feared. If a harmony were nevertheless to creep in, it must be broken immediately or clarified in the philosophical superstructure—with the justification that it is a quotation used to impart even greater impact to the dissonance that follows. Only recently have we again begun to hear young voices who dare to also let beauty resonate through as a result of their work.

The discourse on beauty is probably conducted so intensely and inexorably (to the point of division) in the world of music because it exists only when it is played.

Music exists only for the time when it sounds. This transient circumstance can perhaps best help us to recognize that beauty is not a thing, but a condition. Thus beauty does not exist in isolation, but only in context. That is what makes beauty tangible and desirable in the first place, as moments of experience and life. Its limited duration shows us impermanence, birth, and death.

Over the course of time, a staggering complexity of being has developed through our ceaseless scrutinization of all of nature. The depictions of the resulting problems between nature and us can be reduced to a simple denominator and perceived by us either as a trap or as fantastically simple and therefore beautiful.

"Political considerations are trivial. The leaders of governments throughout the world thought in terms of control, believing power to be the key. [...] The direct nonlinear experience of the brain is communicable. Information passes across the arbitrary boundaries of mankind as though they never existed." (John Brockman)

The sand in this machinery is the incompatible component, the self. A certain vagueness ought to become part of the relation. The keeper of the Grail also says nothing, but unfortunately his silence only inspires the unimaginative who hunger for power.

News Block

As a former president, Bill Clinton tells us that we have to create a world where everyone can be themselves, but where everyone works together. America must lead this development. Jeff Koons, one of the most expensive artists in the world, continually seeks to transgress the boundary of kitsch. Ai Weiwei, the most powerful artist of the greatest dictatorship of work, brings architecture to fruition as a sign of systemic preservation, while in Europe the work is running out.

The CERN collider is the world's largest particle accelerator

In a 27 km long, circular underground tunnel, the smallest known particles are accelerated to nearly the speed of light, sent on a collision course, and brought to collision, smashing them to pieces. In order to detect what happens—whether, for example, even smaller particles are created—gigantic detectors are set up on the site of the planned collision. The goal is to find the theoretically hypothesized smallest subatomic particles as well as dark matter, and all that is measured by the most beautiful of all mathematical formulas, namely the equivalence of mass and energy.

Marking the 70th anniversary

For the expert observers, the sight of the Trinity test must have been intoxicating, beguiling, and horrifyingly beautiful. It was the initial result of the Manhattan Project at the White Sands Proving Grounds in Nevada on July 16, 1945. They immediately transferred the knowledge they gained from the desert to one of mankind's most densely populated areas—blinded by the results of their research. Hiroshima. In retrospect, the ridiculously absurd and impotent attempts by the researchers to claim innocence and provide explanation speak for themselves.

Two Final Speculations

The first: Paradise, as a lost past and the recollection it conjures up, may repeatedly inspire us to dream of a future utopia from a variety of perspectives. Is that perhaps beauty?

The second: Working in collaboration might ignite the spark for recognition of the beautiful. Georg Driendl

5 City

Anonymity prevails as the form of entry into any city of sufficient size. The big city sucks people from the countryside into the city; country in the city. One comes from the country, where all is familiar, and enters the density of the city, a great unknown. It is ruled by laws of division and sharing—for labor, habitation, legal rights, health, and property. Even the water, the air, and the light are tailored and apportioned to a certain extent by statute to the operators, namely the city dwellers. In each relationship arise innumerable interdependencies that assume ever more differentiated forms of communication and coexistence. With no obligation to communicate. Anonymity affords self-fulfillment without history, but necessitates a complex and incontestable administration above it all. The city has long since begun to think of itself as the proof of artificial intelligence; the city dwellers are the switching points.

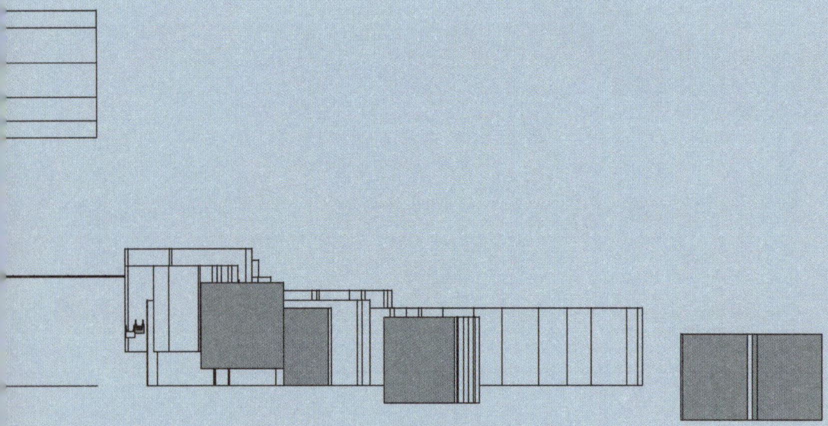

131

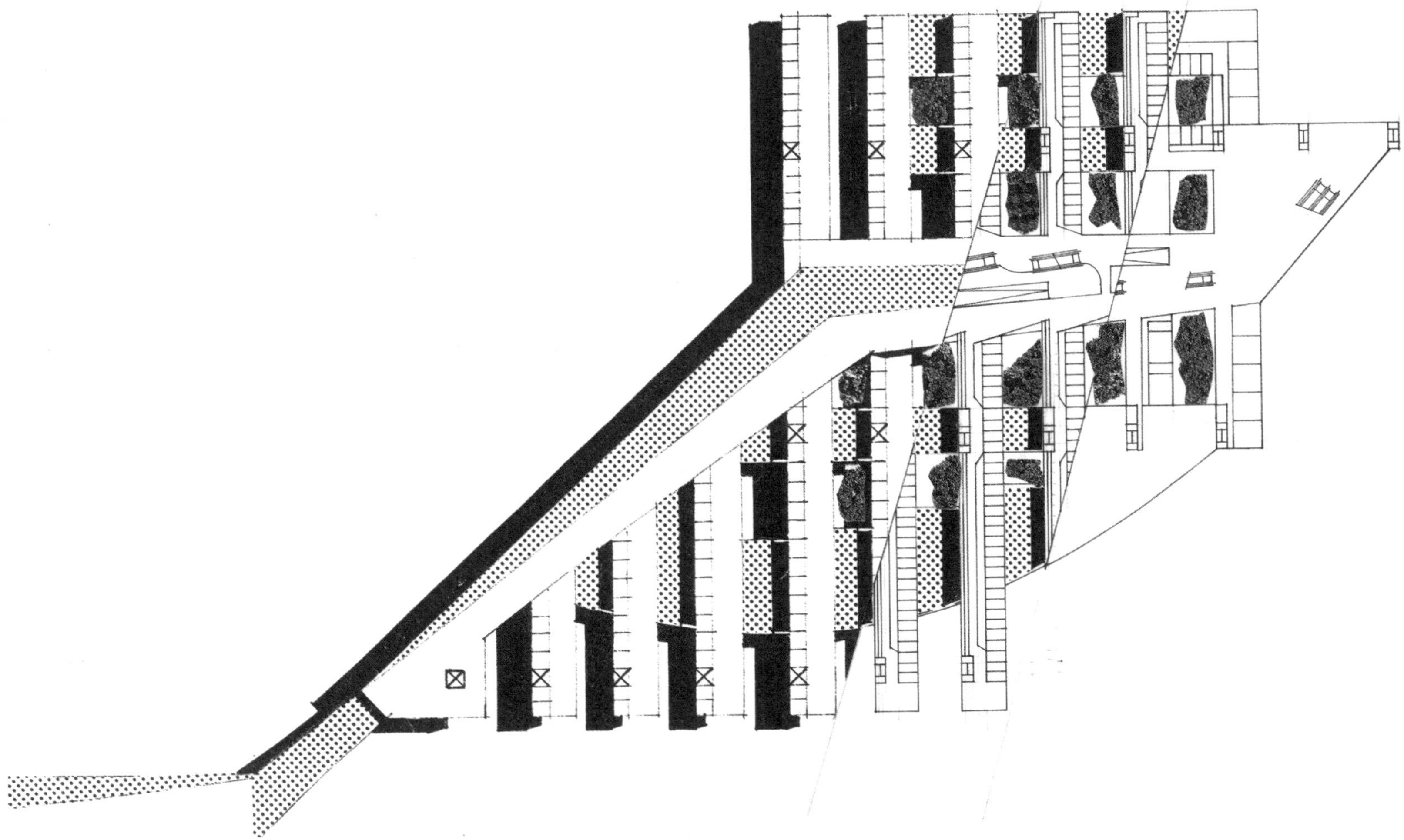

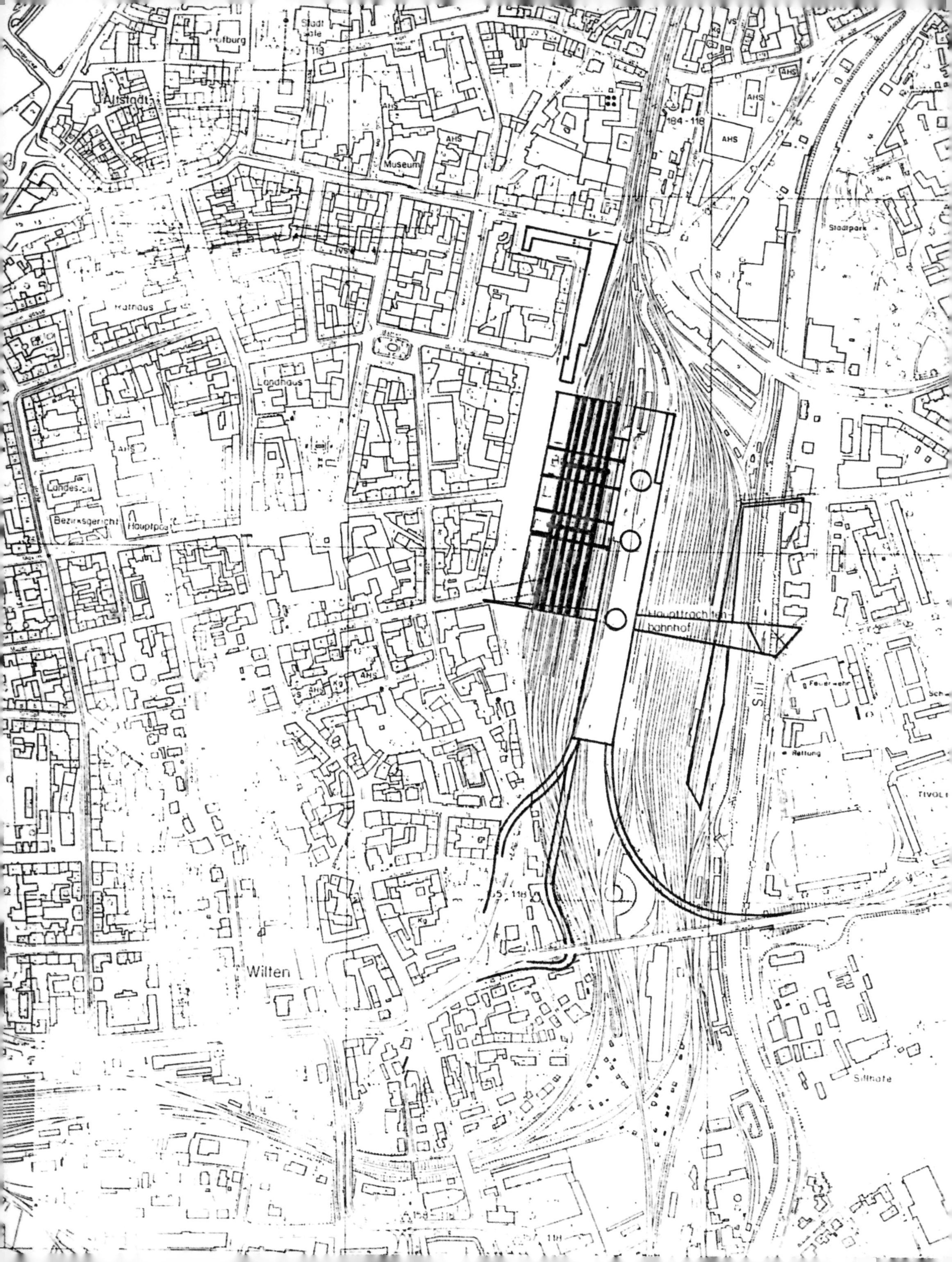
Hofburg
Altstadt
AHS
Museum
AHS
AHS
AHS
Stadtpark
Rathaus
Landhaus
AHS
Bezirksgericht
Hauptpost
bahnhof
Sill
Feuerwehr
Rettung
TIVOLI
Wilten
Kg

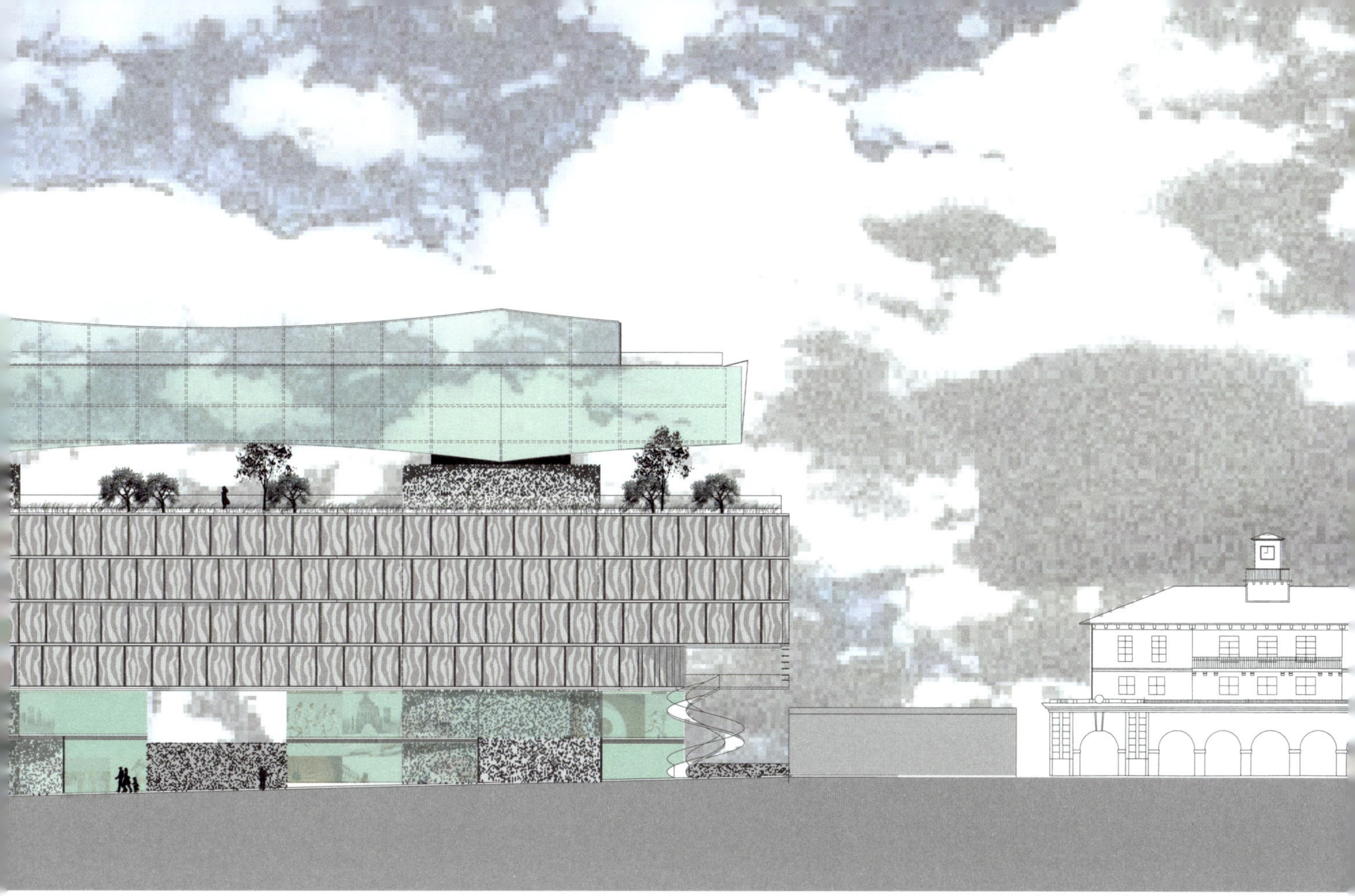
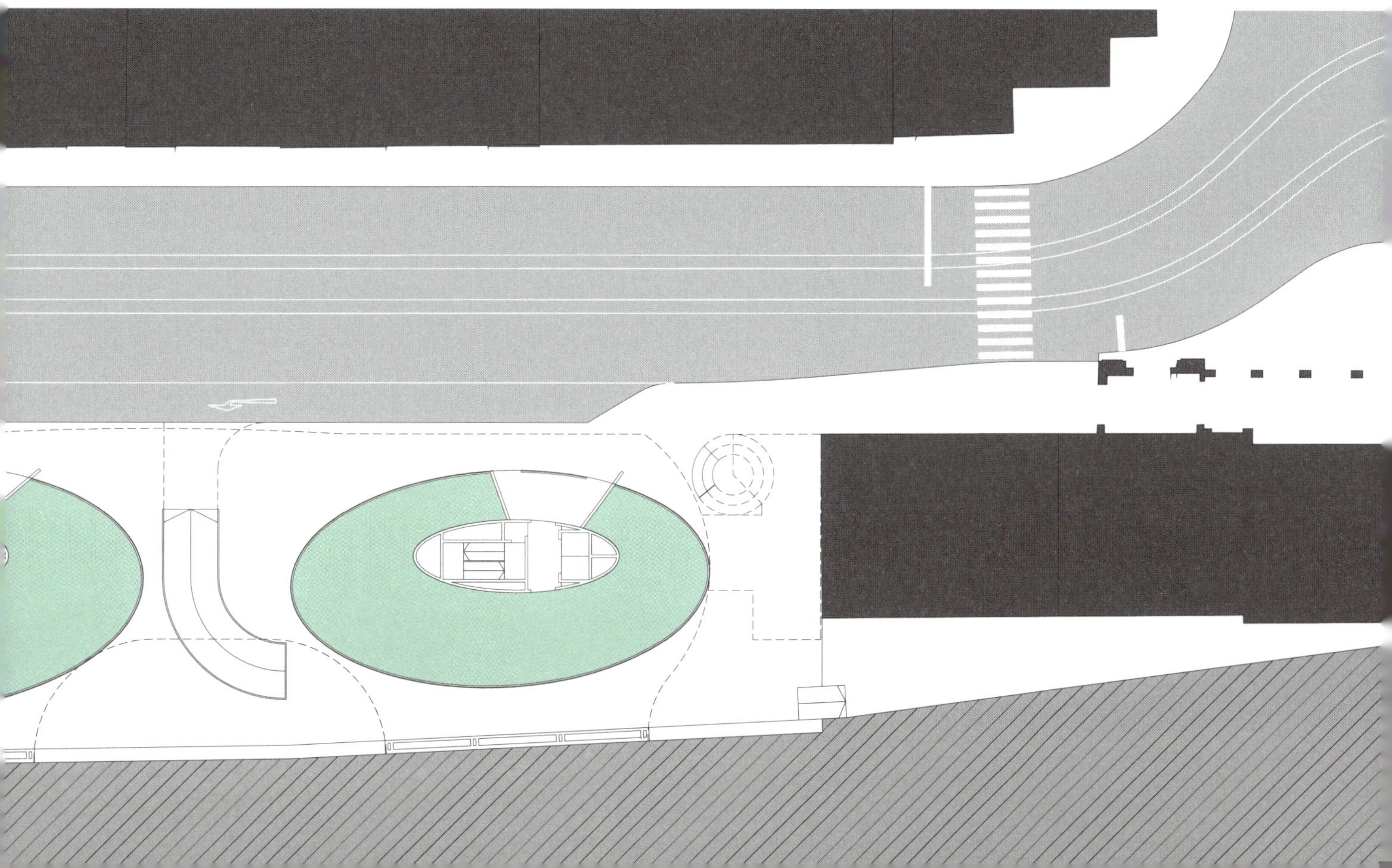

hindrance
isolation
isolation through advertising
post-capital industry - energy saved?
consumption maximized:
dwelling for one
lifestyle for one
agility for one
opinion for all
community hindered

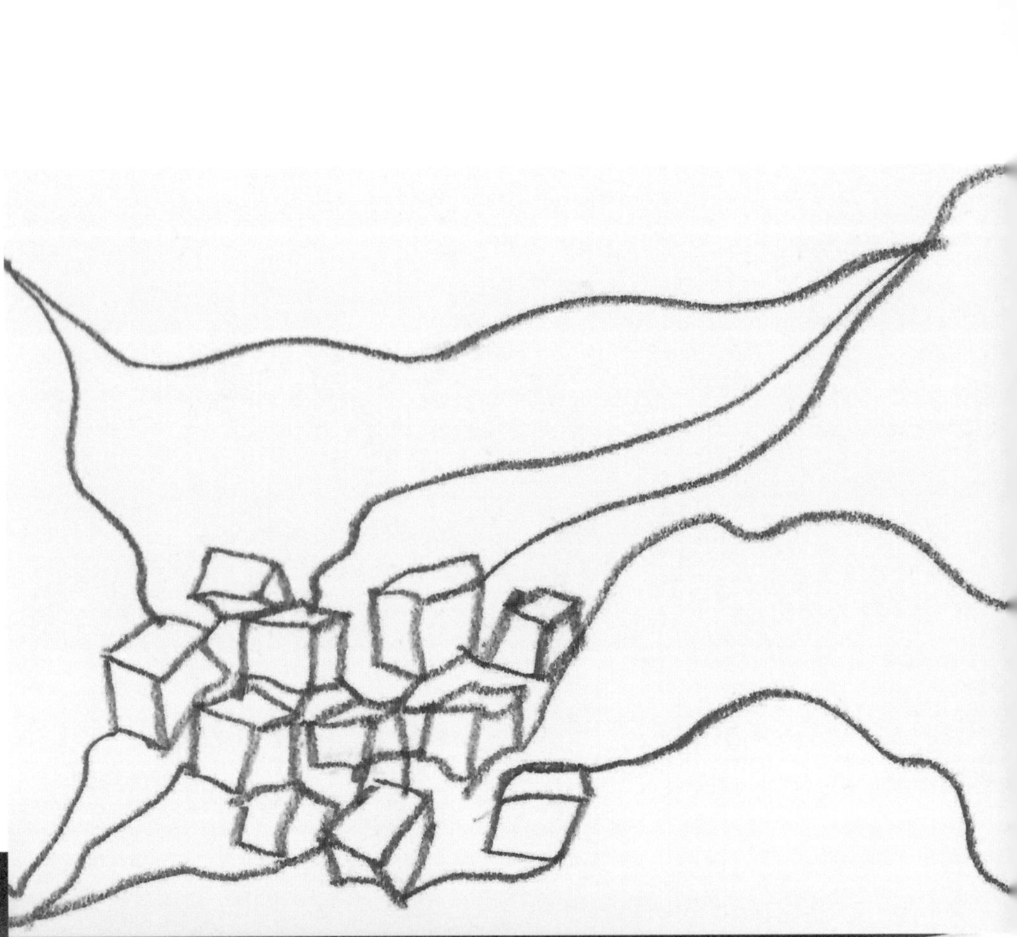

one together two together altogether get-together
you are everyone we are together
all of us are together again, or not?

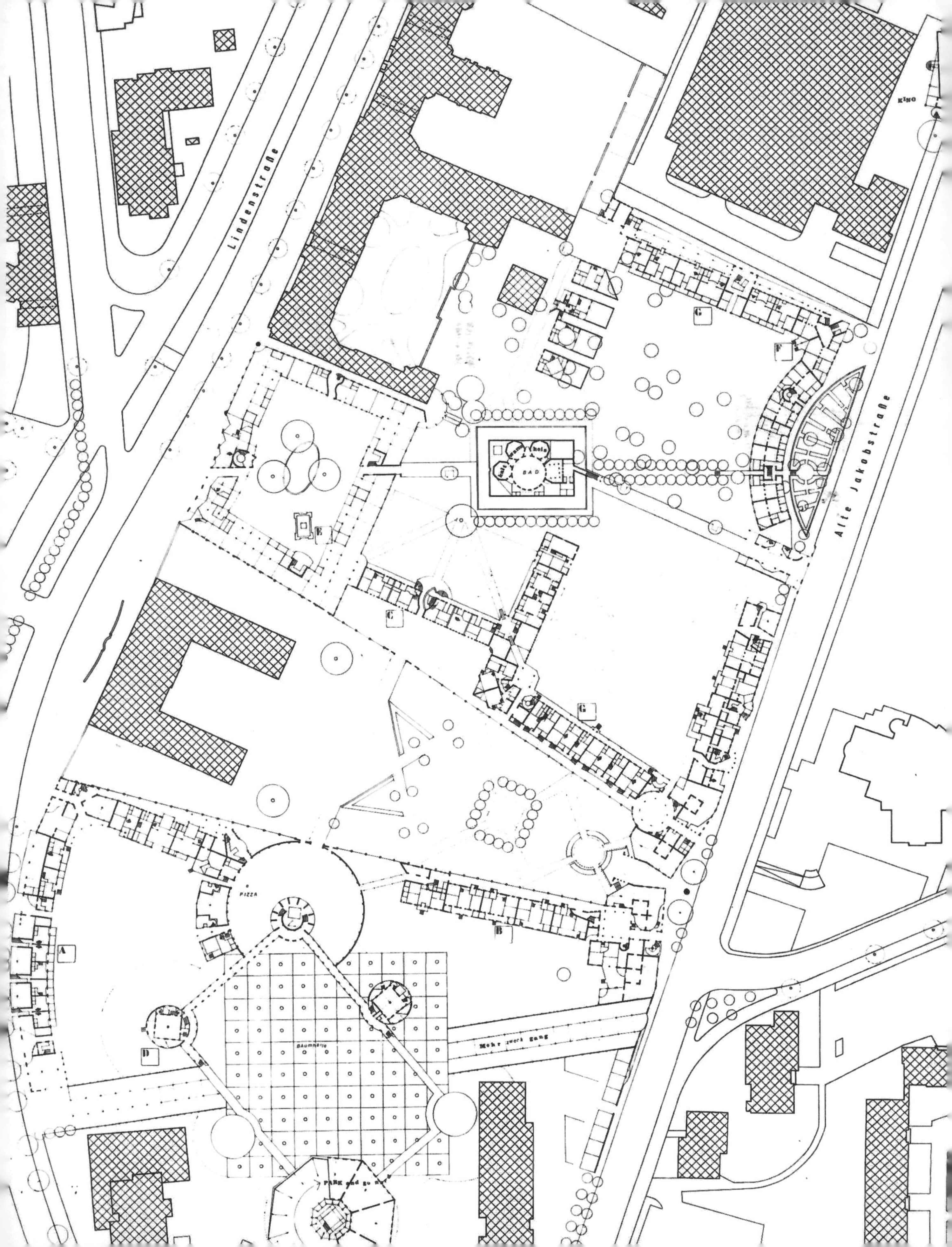
Lindenstraße
KINO
G
F
BAD
Alte Jakobstraße
E
C
G
PIZZA
B
A
D
Mehr zweck gang
Baumhalle

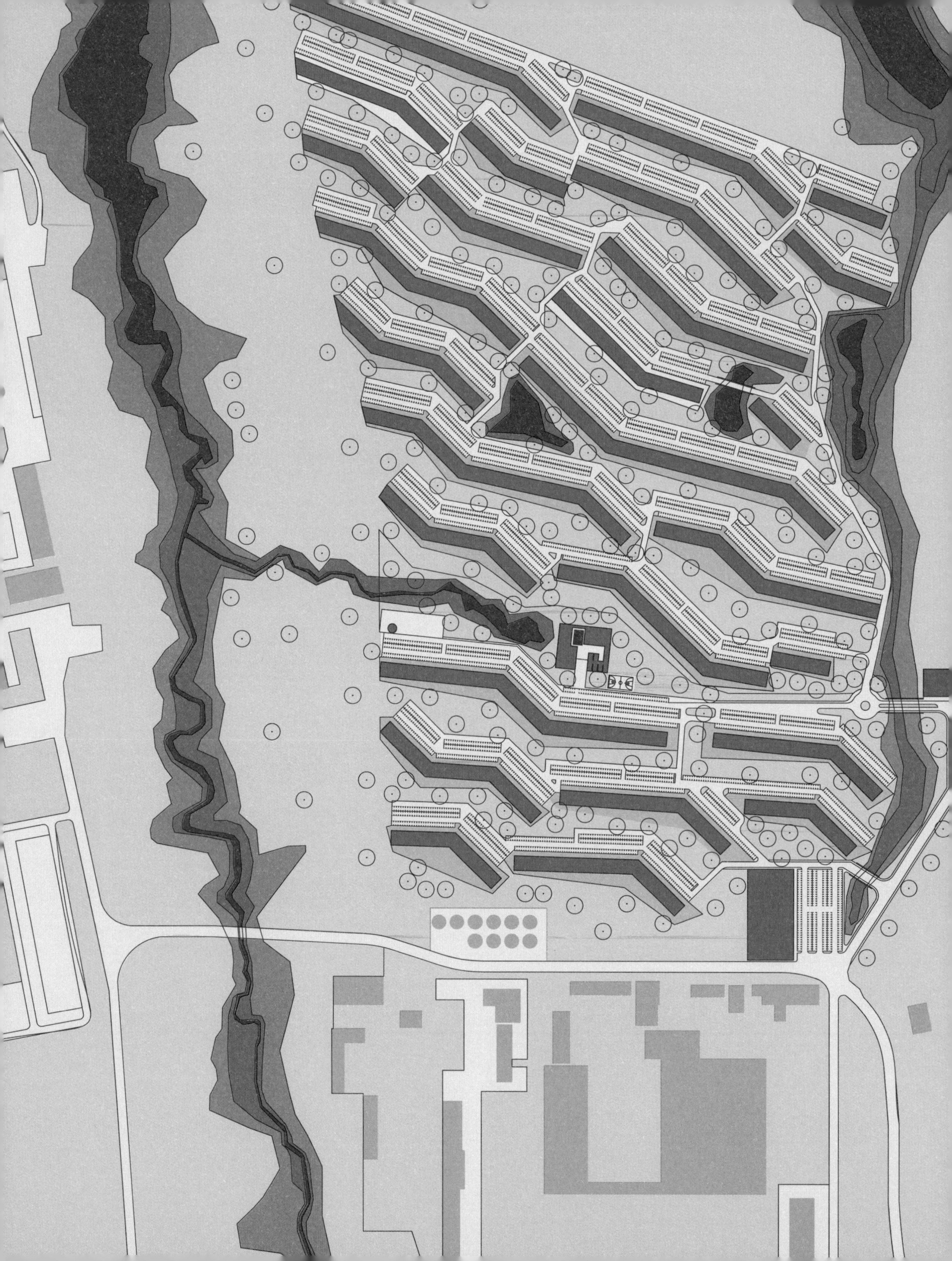

built environment

two categories:
residential and nonresidential
short story
modern industrial smart individualized living
building mass
and not living
produces the city
a mix is the goal
individualized society demands
urban images
a sum of buildings is not enough to make a city
not even a unifying infrastructure is enough to create a city with a sum of buildings
history emerges in the coexistence and superimposition of the old and the new
always
still not a city
city is air displacement

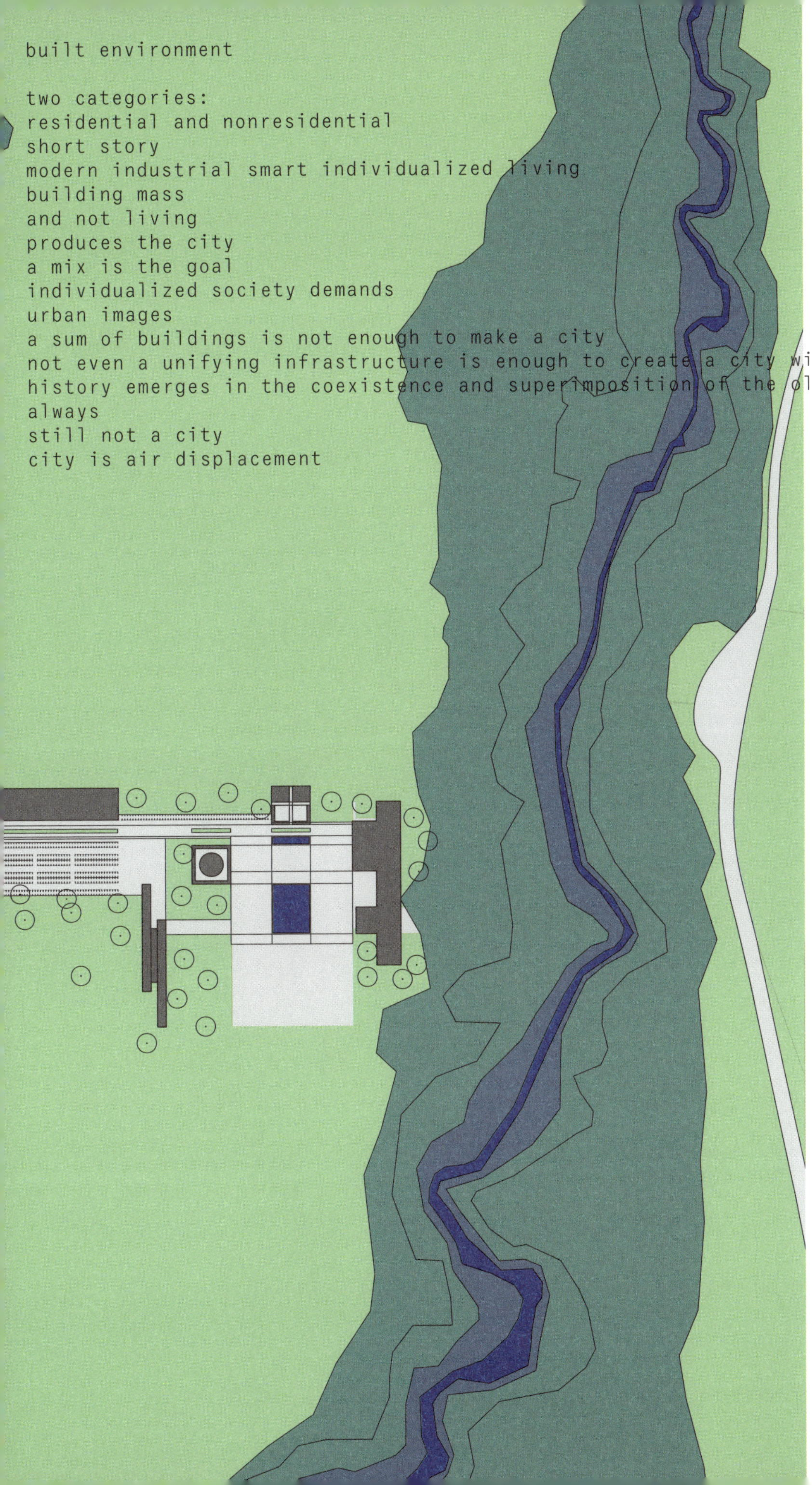

hunt

the brown hare pricks its ears
a quake
a thunder
the direction
projectile approaching
blades of grass are shredded
…

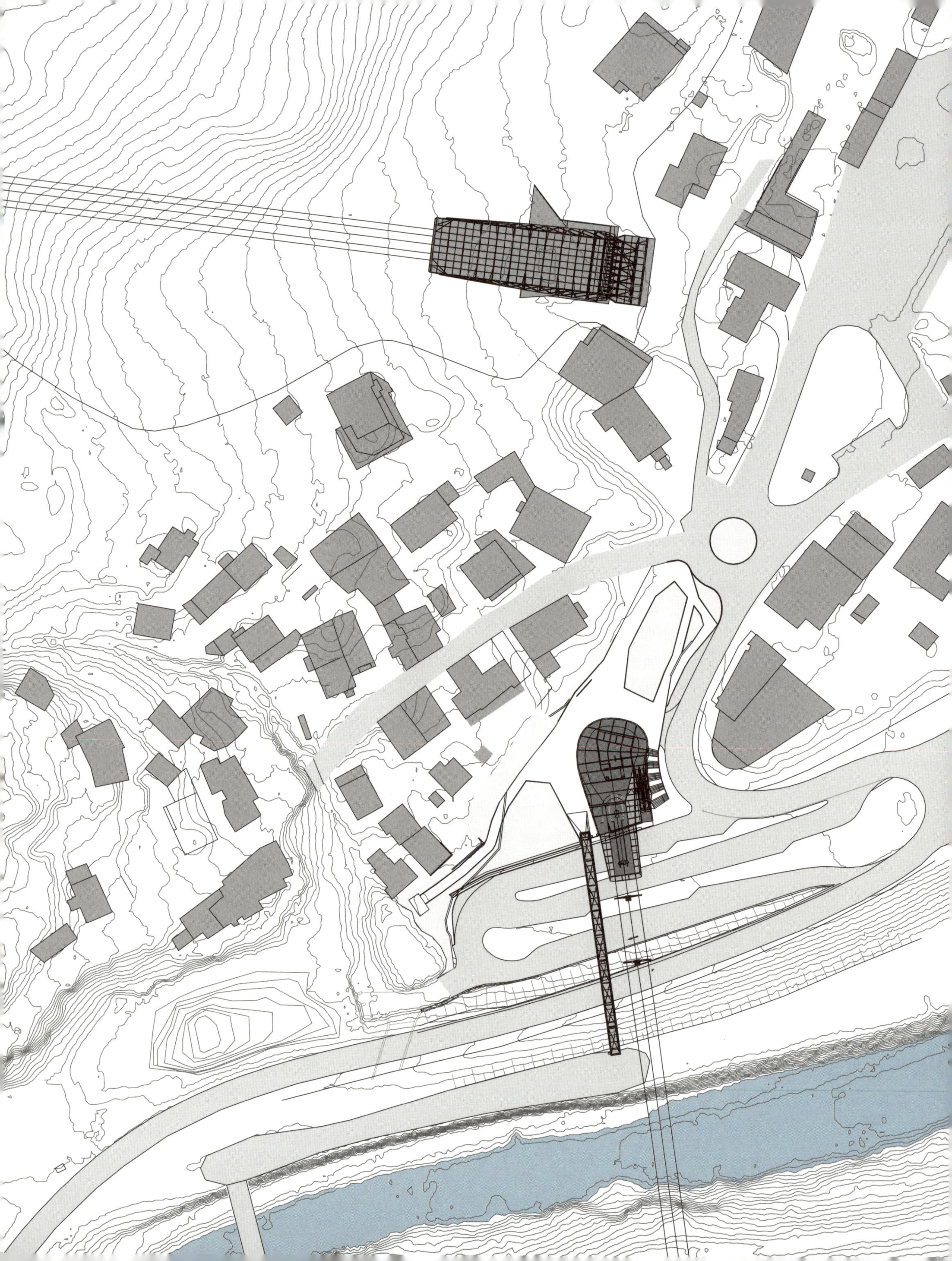

urban development rules

right to air
right to light
right to tranquility
right to protection

neighborhood
common good
design
public before private

rules for freedom
rules for preservation
rules for style and form
rules for infrastructure
rules for development

BRILLEN
KONTAKTLINSEN
D&G

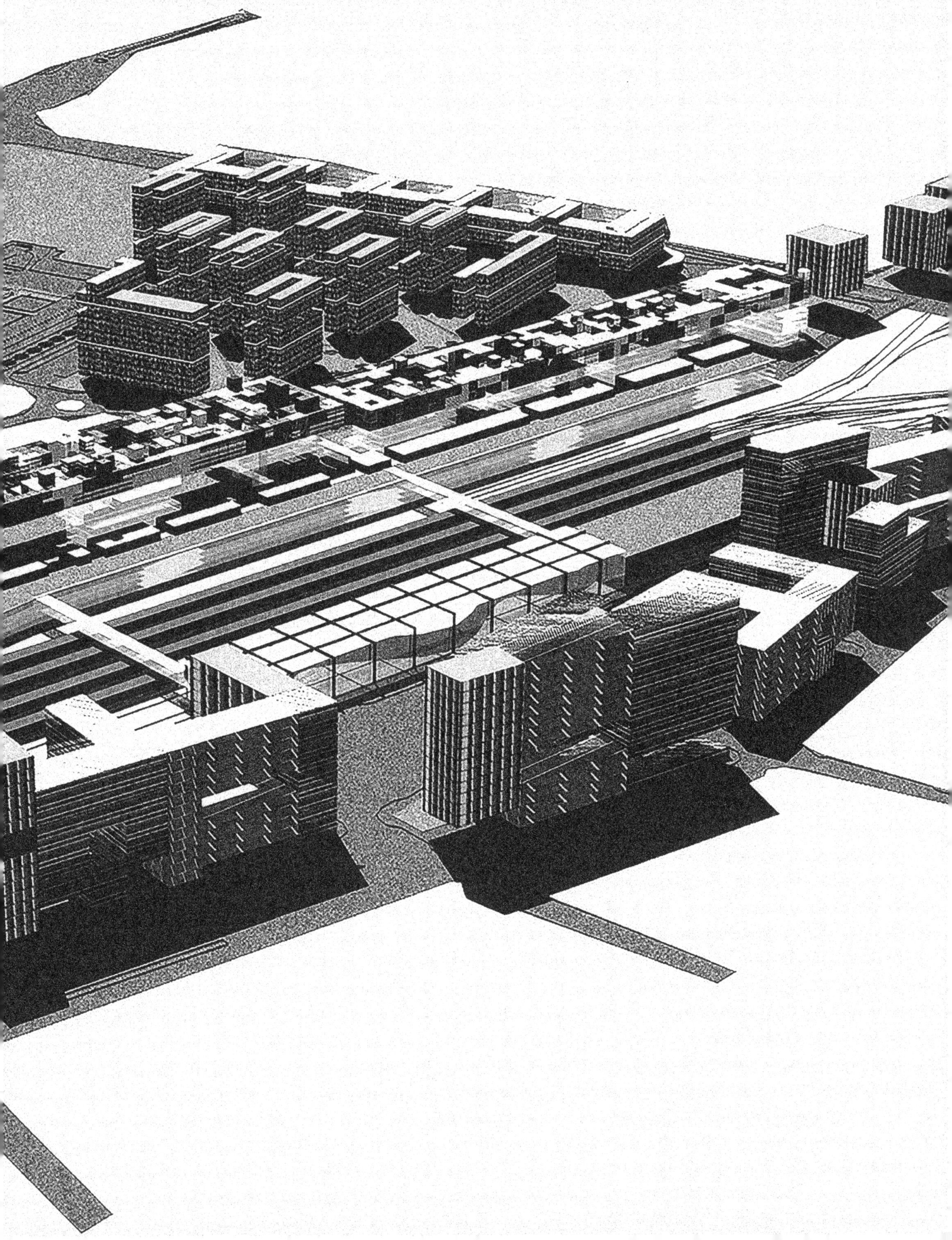

Geometrics

"When a straight line set up on a straight line makes the adjacent angles equal to one another, each of the equal angles is right," says Euclid—using right in the sense of perpendicular, upright.

Perhaps it is a Dadaist room—an "iRoom"—its floor is a mirror, and in the middle, standing upright, is a rod that thus appears in double measure. White light forms the ceiling, and the walls are fantastically dematerialized. The upright human gait—dancing around one's own axis, connected in thought with the center of the Earth—penetrates the world at right angles to the personal horizon.

In Chinese culture, angular measure plays a particularly important role. "Do not do unto others what you would not like to be done unto yourself," says the Book of Rites (Liji) and then continues: "This is what is called 'The Principle with which, as with a measuring square, to regulate one's course.'" The doctrine dates from the time of Confucius, and to this day, one of the most serious insults you could make to a Chinese person is reputedly to say: "You have no measure!" It unforgivingly implies that the decency, righteousness, and sense of justice of the person being addressed are flatly denied.

Aristotle, too, comments in his "Nicomachean Ethics" about the right measure: "the mean relative to us ... by which the man of practical wisdom would determine it. Now it is a mean between two vices, that which depends on excess and that which depends on defect ..."

To quote an old German proverb, "Too little and too much is the goal of all fools" would be the colloquial equivalent. Or, viewed differently: probably only a bad teacher demands mediocrity from his students—thus, measure and mean, but not mediocrity.

Both temporally and practically, the right angle means choosing the shortest path between any one point and a straight line: across a river, for example, or in free fall to the ground. In many newly established cities, where there is nothing present that has developed over time, the so-called Hippodamian system, the rectangular street grid, is a popular solution. This originated in Greek antiquity and is based on the idea of an equal standard for all citizens, the *isonomia*, as a planning principle. The ancient Greek cities of Miletus and Priene, for example, were built on a rectangular grid, as was the Roman Empire city of Augusta Treverorum (now Trier); modern gridded cities we know include Chicago, Washington D.C., and New York City.

The rectangle is bounded by two parallel straight lines, and it accompanies us at every turn: the banknote, the door, a tissue, the endless ream of paper cut along the shortest path endless fanfold paper torn at the perforations—zip!—the right angle is bound to the book; the images on a roll of film, 25 frames per second—whoosh!—cast by a beam of light onto the reflective screen, like at the movies and in front of the monitor; in front of the paintings in the art history museum; sometimes the plates for a multi-course meal at the cafeteria, with four right-angled corners, on a rectangular table that is usually too small; or three-dimensionally: today's Tetra Pak container, misleadingly named and made of coated cardboard, which, when folded accordingly, gives milk a cubic form for efficient delivery. Could all this have developed differently, if it had simply been based on curves or other angles?

Drawing board—the German name (*Reißbrett*) comes from the time before the invention of the graphite pencil, when the draftsman scratched more than drew, using a metal-point stylus called a *Reißblei*. An important feature of the drawing board is its precise angularity, allowing the T-squares and triangles that are used to guide pens or pencils to form a correspondingly exact basis for the drawing coordinates. Design drawings like floor plans, elevations, sections, and perspectives for buildings or machines were, until a few decades ago, put to paper by architects or engineers with T-squares, protractor, triangles, and compasses as well as special technical pens and mechanical pencils. The paper and the pens and pencils have changed over time, but the whole of today's technical environment was developed "on the drawing board" at different scales (drawn at reduced scaled for buildings and technical facilities, and enlarged for machines and electronics). Today, the design (drawing) is created and controlled on a computer monitor using a specially developed program—CAD (Computer Aided Design), for example—by inputting commands that reference preprogrammed paths (aptly gathered in menus), using a keyboard and mouse. The essential difference: there is no scale for creating the drawing; everything is input at full size. The former construction plane of the paper has been replaced by a virtual construction space that is fictive and limitless. Drawings and renderings or other depictions on paper only re-emerge by subsequently plotting them out—as a remembrance, so to speak. Power now lies in sketching, in the hand-drawn sketch. Modeling is done in virtual space. The materials, laws of nature, and energy reserves outside that realm remain unchanged. Programs, logistics, and production methods are constantly renewed and optimized, approaching "one" single hyper-vision. Thus, today we are experiencing a revolution that pertains to more than just a new world or construction method. Perhaps—in all seriousness and without blushing, Monsieur Latour—all the cultural differences on our planet are disappearing at this very moment, namely imperceptibly. Humanity, in what is meanwhile an almost unbounded space of action—without a building block, without a module, and without specifications—is now able to swarm out on the Internet to give form to every vision, in frenzied speed, aided by computer. At the desktop of unlimited possibilities, the question of morality emerges anew as a presumably rudimentary branch of science. Each individual is stronger than ever before, fast moving and highly in demand, yet due to the newly conveyed feeling of omnipresence, also extremely sluggish, like in a dream. Simultaneity, communication at nearly the speed of light, and all ideas together in virtual space—we call that BIM (Building Integrated Modeling), the surface of the computer monitor as a rectangular real-time window to the world. People around the world use the Internet to work on the same model. The data is routed directly into production, moving from CAD for design to CAM (Computer Aided Manufacturing) for fabrication, and the fully automated construction site is guided by satellite and managed via the Internet, on Google Earth corporate servers.

With the Eye of the Drone, an Excursus

The soldier sits in a reclining chair in front of the monitors, looking at highly detailed direct transmissions from the sharp lenses of the cameras of a remote-controlled and heavily armed drone over foreign territory, far, very far away—the target object, a terror cell, is detected—Go! ... For goodness' sake, fractions of a second after issuing the irreversible order to fire, the user (soldier) recognizes children running out of the targeted objective—a school!—It's too late! The missile has been fired and will strike in two seconds, an eternity that remains as a lifelong side effect of reality! A new war without a front—when viewed from the macrocosm, the global political format is surgically precise.

hunt

the hare pricks its ears
a quake
a thunder
the direction
projectile approaching
blades of grass are shredded
...

With these new instruments and the consequences and impacts associated with them, people are now truly at the center of everything, and what's more, they must remain the measure of all things and, in the social networks, first find the right proportion in dealing with this technology: inner stability and inner balance: Know thyself!—The "iPhon(ician)".

After an exhibition opening in Venice, a group of us walk through an alley perpendicular to the dockside. A large yacht moves by slowly. Its crewmembers pose proudly on deck, facing their observers. At this moment, a much larger yacht comes into view. The crew of the first yacht stand about until someone, perhaps due to the astonished faces of the observers, turns around and recognizes: the onlookers' attention is focused on the yacht behind them. Those who had been posing immediately disappear below deck. The scene disbands. The right measure still exists!

As a planner on the project "non-profit housing"—"social housing" has been purged from decorous common usage—one can try to develop a useful canon for needs-oriented, low-cost housing beyond fashionable trends. One can also generally try to meaningfully influence the design of the built or not yet built environment, namely in terms of social, health, and evolutionary aspects to be, in short, humane. The motive would simply be responsibility.

The media reported a horrendous mass murder in a housing complex in northern Italy. A man in a state of panic had extinguished the lives of all the adjacent neighboring families—those living above, below, and next-door—with an automatic firearm. It was determined that what triggered his panic was simply insufficient soundproofing between the apartments, and the resulting stress from the noise over a long period of time.

Building is not done alone, but always together, within a society that seeks to build something up. The social relationships in a social network, such as respect for neighborship, can be constructive for this purpose. But if living becomes a commodity, what then? An advertisement from a Turkish illustrated magazine serves as a good example: The tag line written in big letters across a double-page photomontage reads, "live above dreams." Above in the picture we see an enormous residential development, and below is an empty movie theater—what a soaring start!

In his film "Playtime," Jacques Tati gives us a scene with a bus full of tourists slowly driving past a large display window, reflecting the passengers inside the bus. At that very moment, a window cleaner tilts the display window, causing all the occupants of the bus to heave a deep sigh of surprise and relief as the mirror image is tilted away. Yes, of course. Now they see things from a familiar angle.

The act of building is age-old and also a metaphor: Today we not only build houses, machines, networks, and airplanes—that is, flying houses—but in a philosophical sense we also build up dreams, hopes, and illusions for the individual, who is in a position to act freely throughout the world. To protect this luxury, we are simultaneously building up human rights as a regulating mechanism for the coexistence of all these things—until war once again destroys everything, if the right balance can no longer be found between the individual in society, on the one side, and nature and an unleashed technology on the other. Artists function as seismographs for stability, and in the museum, all that remains is just a memory; the future does not exist. Art is now, only now. Georg Driendl

walk on egg shell's story

6

Plaything

Are you just playing around? If yes, then give me that special something I need to join in the fun. Children are straightforward. They'll have a thought, and with it a question, and with any question with no answer comes the problem. Children play. Just like that. Play is entertainment—or is playing doing, without really doing something? No, play is dangerous, murderous; especially when the players are not children. Without rules, the things we play with can be hellish stuff. But with discipline and by keeping the other players in mind it becomes entertainment, maybe even a path to learning, a way to sketch out, invent, plan, and organize life that has not yet been experienced. On paper or as a thing, before heads roll because of misunderstandings. But we are in the game and mighty proud of how our fellow players understand us, even though we sometimes fail to bring along high spirits ...

sparkling reception

by foot or faster

origin xyz

safe landing

walk-over

suspended trust

big brother

shape deck

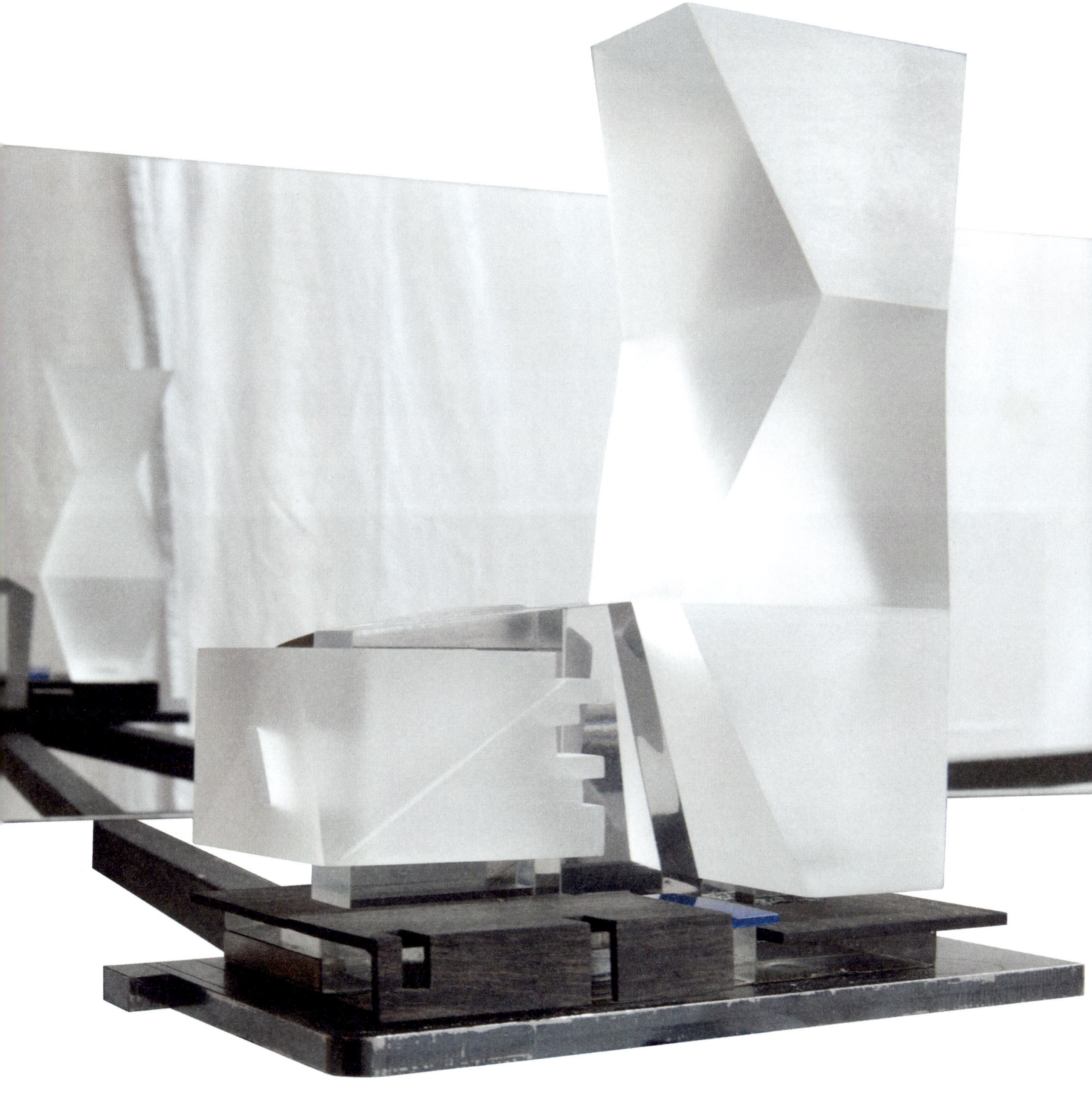

cold opposition

the curve and the bend

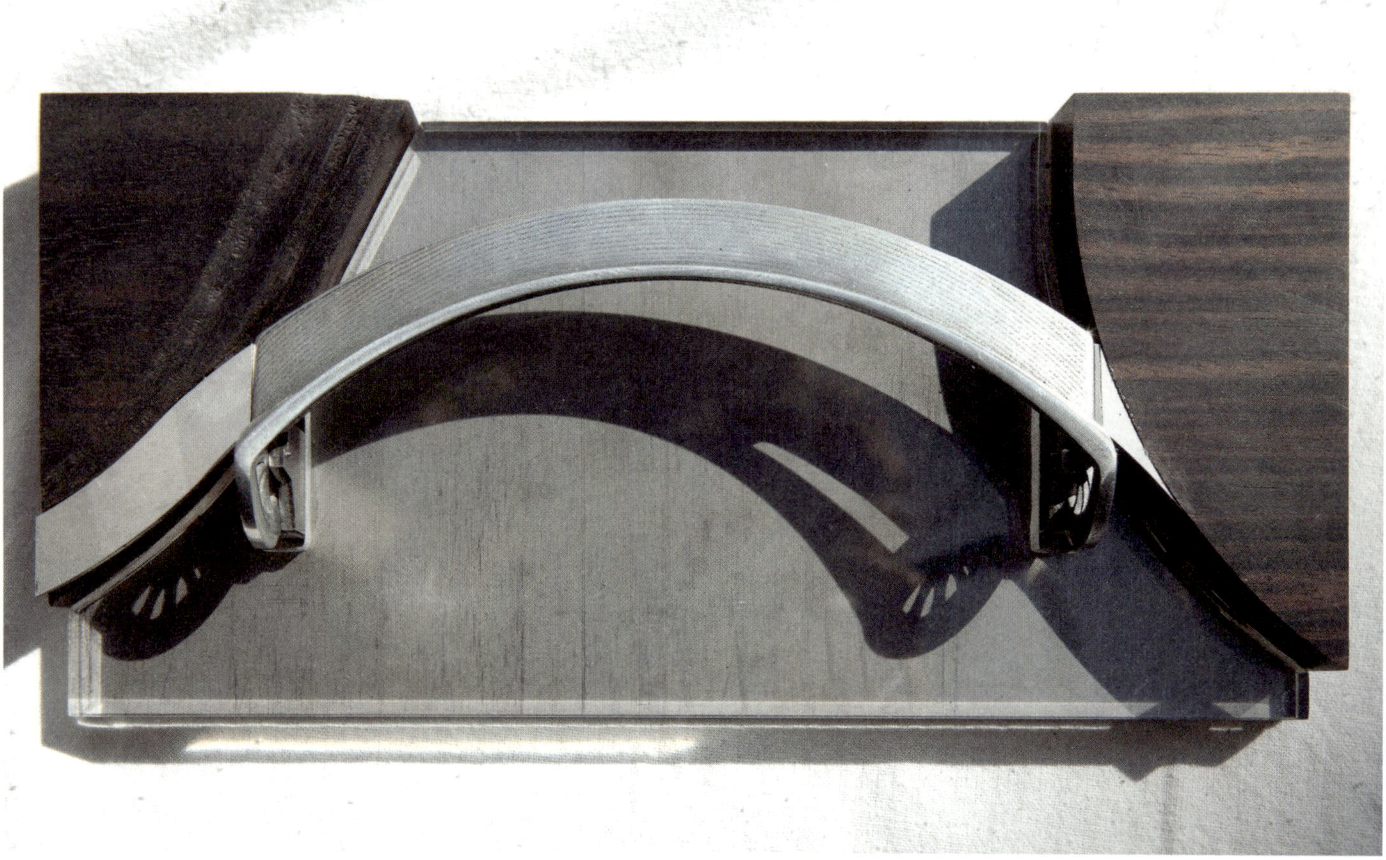

crystal rank-growth

hoverfront

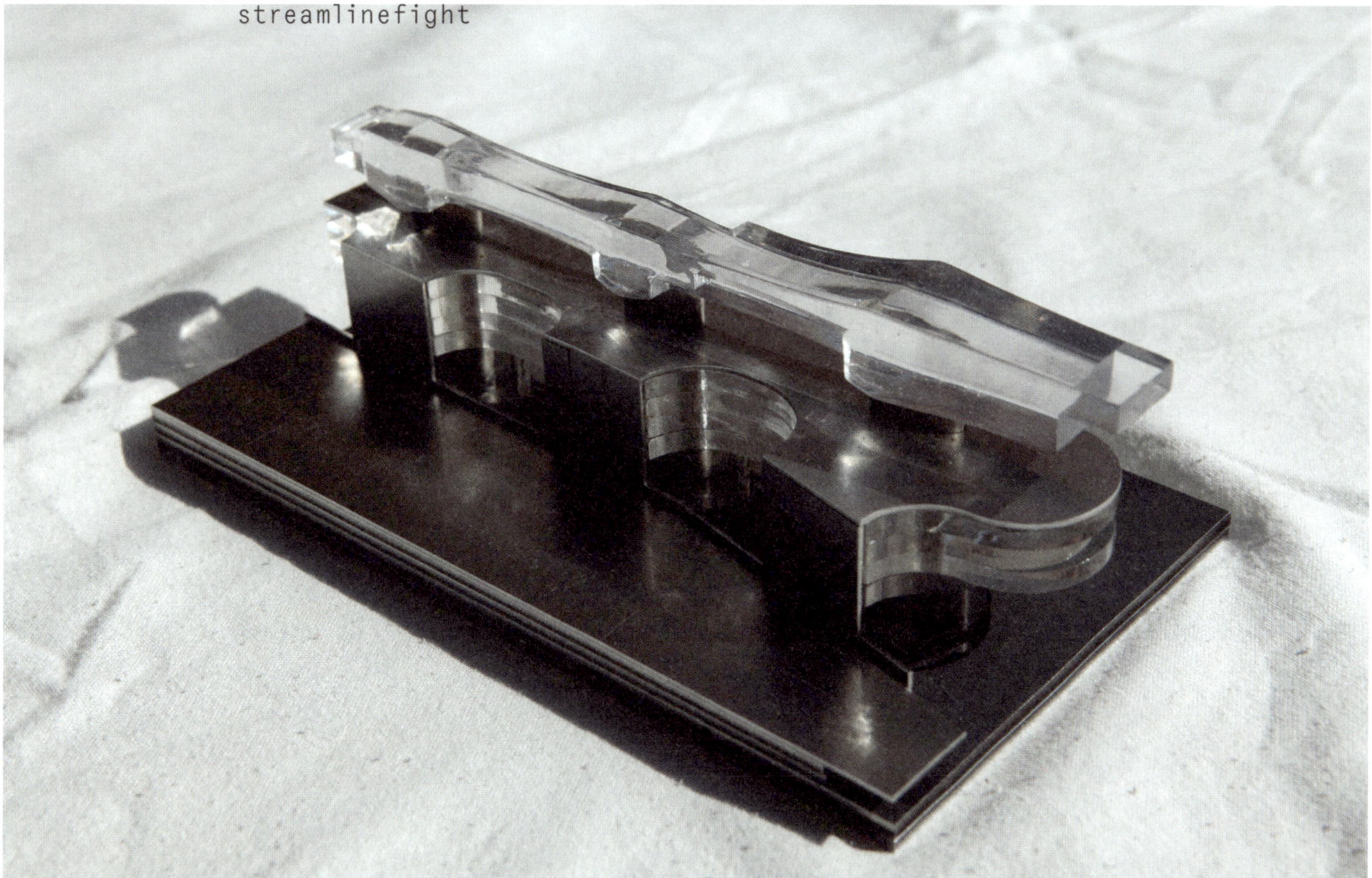
streamlinefight

parallel jamed

closed circle

ground zero

O Fighter: Hello

Carlene: An open position!

Margarete: Our company needs employees

Amalie: Give attention to our job offer

Gudrun: It's about your interview for the new position

Magdalene: The position of chief manager is available

Hedy: The interview is scheduled for tomorrow!

Swanhilda: You have to go through the job interview to get the new post

Swanhilde: Send your résumé

Waltraud: We haven't found your résumé. Please send it again

Waldburga: You have been appointed to the new position

Helmine: It's a disgrace to earn as little as you do

Wills: I'm tired of writing to you. Is the work even necessary?

Carla: Your application was rejected. You're an idiot!!

Erdmut: There's a new job opening!

Adeltrudis: A vacant position

[illegible]: Read the letter that changes your life.

Emmeline: Everyone who reads this letter becomes rich!

Herrick: That's how smart people work

Heilwig: I made a million a week without any risk!

Liesel: I like to share with you effective ways to earn money

Wilbert: We want to offer you work

Adelonda: By dawn you can rise to become a rich man

Hermann: It's about your interview for the new position

Sigiswald: But you can also spend Valentine's Day in my bed

Ottokar: The interview is scheduled for tomorrow!

Tenado: We will help you advance, Georg Driendl!

Lewenhart: No complicated and monotonous work anymore! Let the robot work for you!

Walburg: You sleep. The program earns money!

Reinilde: Change your life right now! There won't be another chance!

Amalia: By dawn you can rise to become a rich man

Sonje: Money brings you freedom, power, and beautiful women!

Wilfreda: Machinery devoid of feeling is working for you, you're getting richer and richer!
My bank account keeps growing bigger day by day! That's a pleasant surprise!

The secret of earning REAL money has finally been revealed!

WA: CONGRATULATIONS You have won $6,500,000.00 US.

Kirsa: Will you marry me?

Franziska: I want to be next to you.

Luna: Why are you so poor?

Severin: I suggest a new job.

Waldobert: Our getting together will be the best thing that ever happened to you.

Clarimond: My friend earns $100,000 an hour without getting up from the chair!

Sascha: He who has money has everything, don't you agree?

Sigi: Your silence confuses me a little.

Ricarda: Don't write to me anymore if you won't open the letter.

Hlludowig: Either you answer me or I'll go away.

Selina: I must leave you, goodbye and farewell!

Gundula: It's a pleasure to see you again. Wow, gorgeous vehicle!

the pleasure calling of the airhead
call out what he likes to hear!
it has an elegant allure
how he consumes it
amid the admirers
proudly breaded
his head protrudes above the decor
all honor he pretends
has he nothing, he'll just make styrofoam amends

genmanipulierte
architektur
parasite drill

HOTEL
EINGANG

KASSA 1
KASSA 2

ideowall frucade oder eierlikör
factory kleines frühstück
kinderterrarium antipasti
seppelerstube
boarder rooms
massage solarium

here and there

u
are
who are you
what do you have
what are you doing
(hush)
look at me

u
are
who are yu
what do yu have
watcha doin’
(shh)
look at me
well

when the moonlight doesn’t shine
the lion growls, and then – who knows?
the gull has an idea
you decide, says the deer
so now who’s lion, gull, or deer?

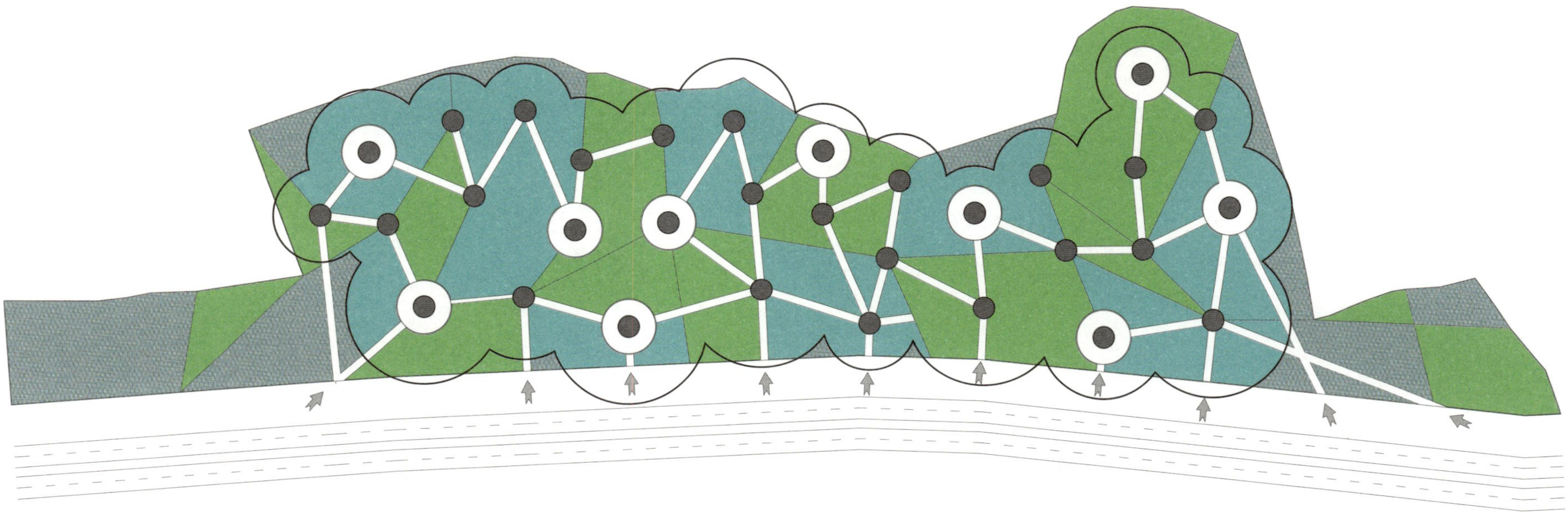

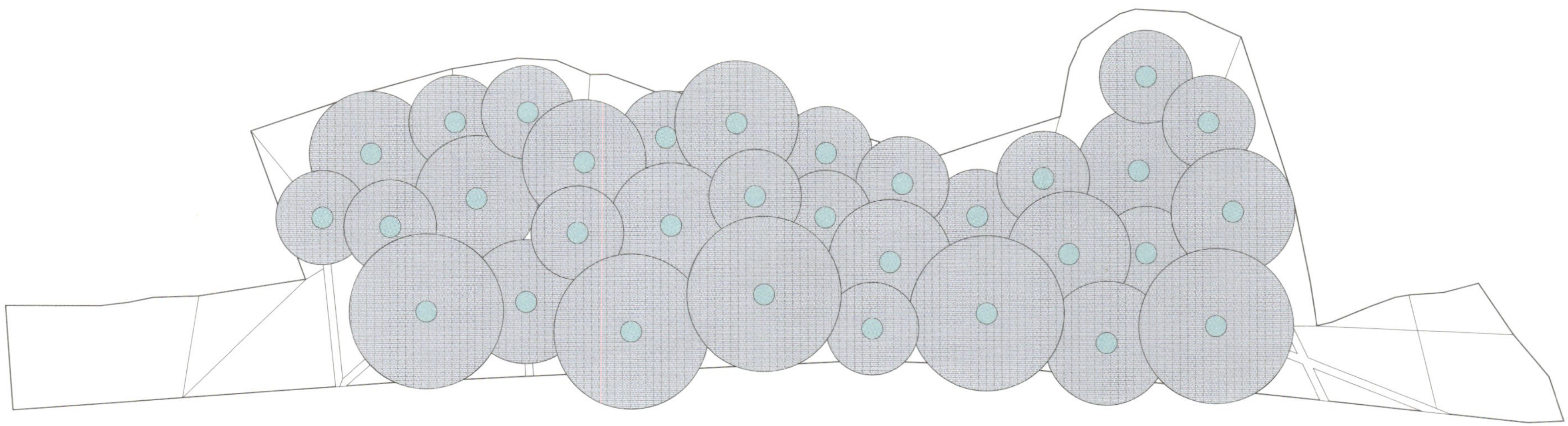

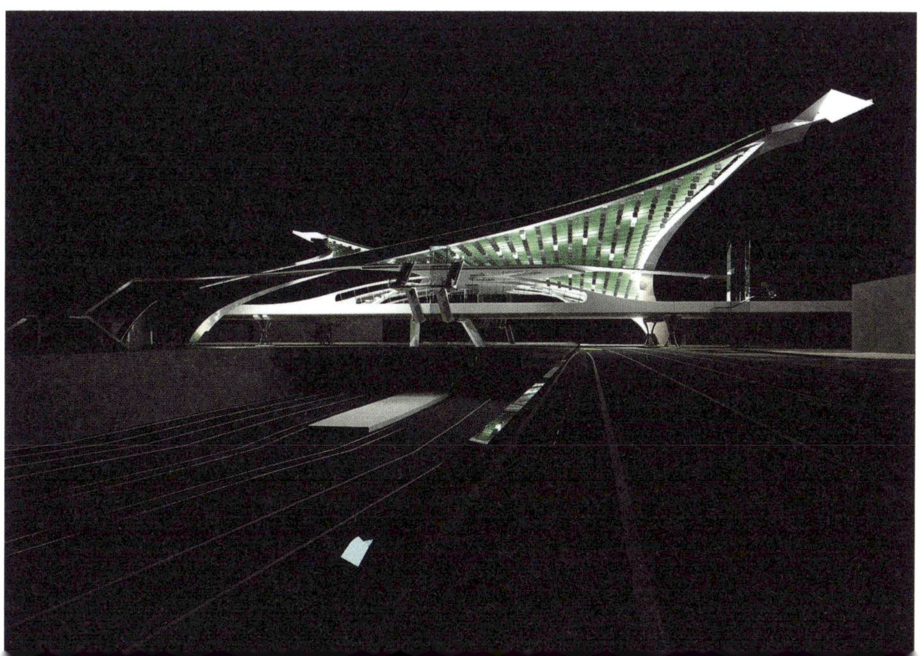

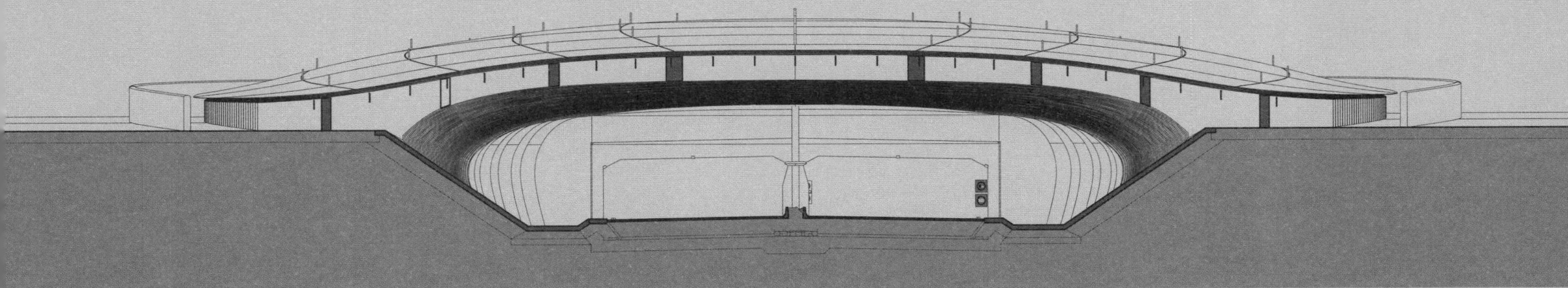

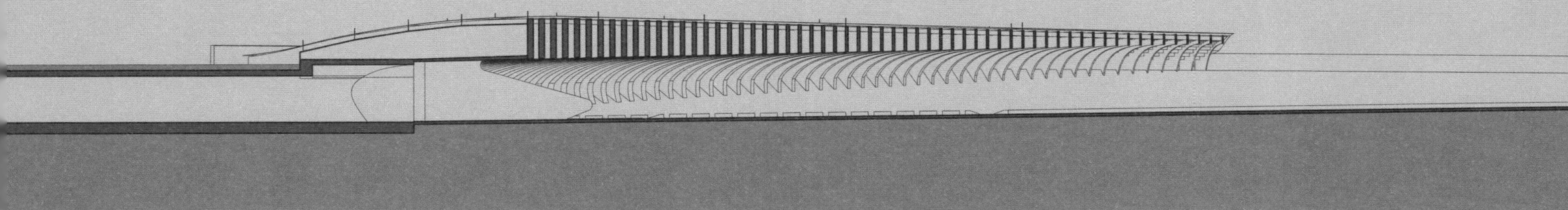

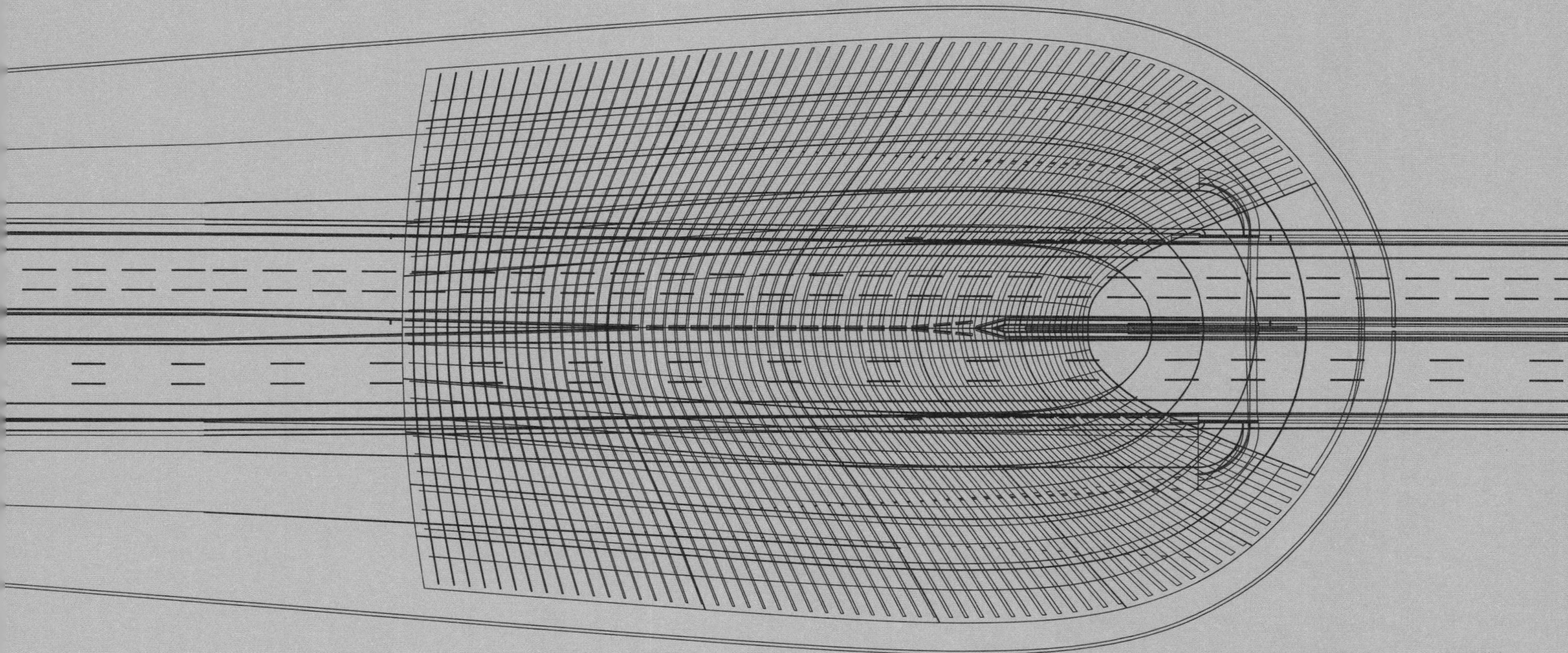

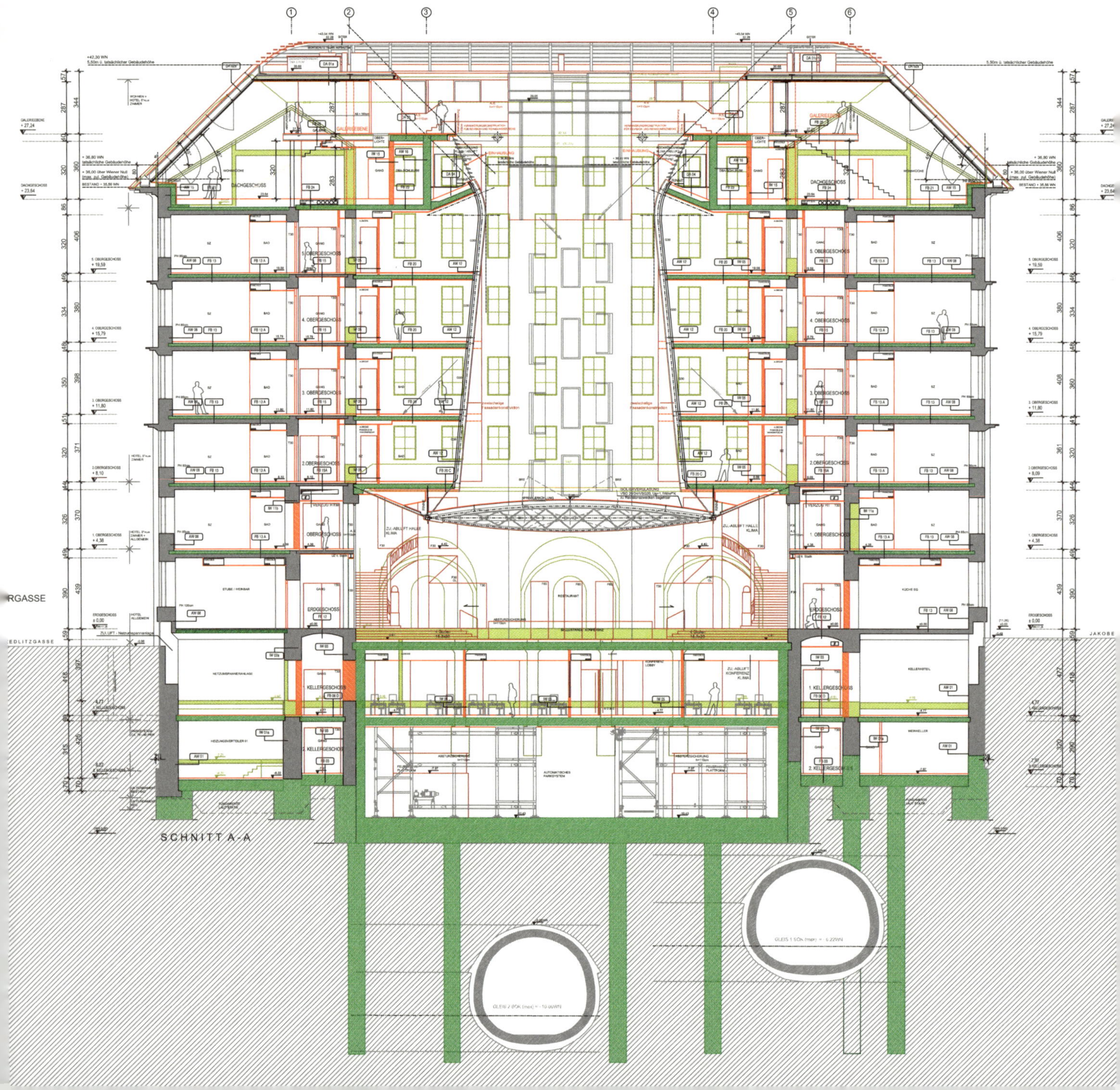
SCHNITT A-A
RGASSE
EDLITZGASSE
JAKOBE
DACHGESCHOSS
5. OBERGESCHOSS
4. OBERGESCHOSS
3. OBERGESCHOSS
2. OBERGESCHOSS
1. OBERGESCHOSS
ERDGESCHOSS
KELLERGESCHOSS
2. KELLERGESCHOSS
GALERIEEBENE
RESTAURANT
AUTOMATISCHES PARKSYSTEM

thankful
for a successful escape
fear
of serene confidence
courage
to reflect openly
struggle
for the idea

A Fleeting Thought in Advance about Cities ...

In the face of nothingness, it would be naive to believe to be omniscient. Who are we? Ability is doing. What? One sticks to the other; we love being close. All of humankind is crowding into the cities, dense, denser; the denser, the better. Millions and tens of millions in the struggle to build up subtle differences. Everyone is working on nurturing idiosyncrasies so that something is going on, namely the city. Many, as many as possible. This tumult first lulls us into a cozy mood, swimming amongst the masses.

The land is now only roamed by lonely wolves. Everything is in the city. The countryside is becoming a deserted province, a utopia for the dreams of city dwellers, a projection. Crowds, shoulder to shoulder, jostling, scrutinizing each other's wardrobes, feeling the thrust of their bodies. Submerge, emerge, run alongside, ahead, behind. The movement is amplified by another next to, above, and below you; everything is crazy, night and day. There's no standstill, not even when things slow down. Instead, the pushing gets that much stronger. Seeing, the blink of an eye, the shrug of the shoulders, the squinting in the midst of it all—always in full concentration. Nobody knows anybody. Everyone is at home. Like in the village, but anonymous. Anonymity, but otherwise like at home. Growth has no limits. Expanding collectively. An urban body. The cell is bloated and excites upon contact with the others. The bursting, when it happens, is to be perceived but centrally registered. Observers become the observed and witnesses of mistakes, but the code is correct. The crook steals the scene, a handkerchief, international capital. But from where?—this question is not raised. The city mutates into a big city. A garrulous vocabulary continually practices new strategies. Languages confuse, the communication on the periphery, the middle is tradition. Clearly knowing: There are also other big cities.

The city is becoming a landscape. Landscapes have grown, and done so naturally, without interest in those who want to settle here and make their mark. No place is naturally the way it is, but develops instead along the lines set out by the nature that spawned it. Or is our constant companion, technology, not nature? Regardless: What is nature? What is science? The natural city, or better, the natural big city—or even better: the natural global city. That is our place of dwelling, not the Arctic, the ocean, or the Himalayas. Those are places where adventure seekers seek stillness and silence. We are urbanites.

Cult and culture are stowed away behind facades. The museum, the rearview mirror. We find our affinity in the favorable opinion of the neighbor. Many seekers; like-minded people, but hardly compatible. Science explains, details are added and honed; for the time being we know everything. We need to be clear about what we want to do with all our stuff, or what we want to continue doing with what has already been begun. If we ask ourselves whether the multiplication table is correct or if it only simulates a certain idea of an anachronistic order, we come again and again to the same conclusion. It is impossible to make irrevocable assertions, and it is possible to change everything, even one's imagination.

In the city and its intrinsic surroundings, about which we are pleased, which are important to us, and which allow us unimagined realities, we recognize diversity and the simultaneous validity of juxtaposition and superimposition.

The intimacy of this neighborhood sometimes turns work into leisure and frees it from necessity, thereby establishing a relative ease in dealing with the natural problematic of existence. Precisely this form of existence is a fundamental prerequisite for urban life; we are permitted to wish for functions here. Our ability to fulfill these desires demands the readiness to accept nothing as given. The professional is superior to the dilettante in terms of approach, and conversely, the dilettante outshines the professional with a non-predictable, undaunted way of moving on; in a sense a mutant. City dwellers are dilettante mutants. At least a little, at any rate.

Simultaneously, there are a wide variety of invisibly acting rules.

Ultrafast media-disseminated systems, ways of looking at the world, systems of order, norms, and laws are superimposed with impenetrable complexity by that which has been historically passed down, time-honored traditions, and the modern. The result is an impenetrable jungle of mixed notions that accumulate additively and unendingly, like a creeping transformation that is ceaselessly fueled and changed from within. Our clear view of the essential is obstructed. Perhaps that is why we have learned to love the unexpectedly fragile, the inessential, the practical joke, and the embellishment.

According to Euclid's fifth postulate, "if a straight line falling on two straight lines makes the interior angles on the same side less than two right angles, the two straight lines, if produced indefinitely, meet on that side on which are the angles less than the two right angles." This was already considered unaesthetic in ancient times and remained unresolved for 2,000 years. The parallel postulate suddenly became invalidated at the speed of light when Einstein's Theory of Relativity gave us the explanation of how space-time is curved. Despite that, if I visualize two circles, with one center with an infinite radius, the circular segments discernable from my perspective are straight and parallel.

The World.

"But indeed, to the palpably sophistical proofs of Leibniz that this is the best of all possible worlds, we may seriously and honestly oppose the proof that it is the worst of all possible worlds. For possible means, not what one may construct in imagination, but what can actually exist and continue. Now this world is so arranged as to be able to maintain itself with great difficulty; but if it were a little worse, it could no longer maintain itself." (Arthur Schopenhauer).

One's own will is reality, and appearance is mere imagination. The negation of will is one way to overcome the boundaries of imagination, the boundaries between me and you.

Our Spaceship Earth is the place of origin of all known life forms, 4.6 billion years old, 12,700 km in diameter, approximately spherical, 5.9 × 1024 kg in weight, 5.5 g/cm^3 mean density, rotates around its own axis in 23 hours 56 minutes and 4.9 seconds, along an elliptical orbit at a speed of 29.78 km/s in 365 revolutions around its own axis per year, once around the sun.

The atmosphere is composed of nitrogen, oxygen, argon, and aerosols (carbon dioxide, neon, helium, methane, hydrogen, nitrous oxide, carbon monoxide, ozone); it is light but heavier than nothing and thins as one moves out to its periphery. On the outer crust, between the air and matter that is more solid, prevail a pressure of 1.014 bar and maximum temperatures of minus 89°C to plus 58°C, depending on the topography.

The sphere's 510 million km^2 of surface area is perceived by us, as we cleave to the ground or float on the water thanks to gravity, as an up and a down beneath the sky. Water accounts for two-thirds of the surface area and land one-third—for the time being. Thanks to the metabolism of plant life—in other words, photosynthesis—the earth's atmosphere was enriched with molecular oxygen and thus gained its oxidizing nature.

We estimate that the ongoing process of biochemical evolution has been underway for 1.9 billion years thus far. Bearing that in mind, the climate changes we are currently observing are happening at a breathtaking pace, accelerated by the greenhouse gas effect caused by carbon dioxide emissions into the atmosphere. The impact of these dynamics, set into motion by us, is unpredictable and could dramatically, and above all, very quickly, change the living conditions here on

Earth. The mass of our planet consists mainly of iron, oxygen, silicon, magnesium, sulfur, nickel, calcium, and aluminum. Irrespective of how we continue to develop, the future of our spaceship is tied to the nature of the sun. The nuclear fusion processes taking place there will increase its overall brightness by 10% in the next 1.1 billion years and by 40% after 3.5 billion years. These processes mean that the Earth can only remain populated by us for about another 500 million years. This dynamic is inescapable and irreversible, so we should not worry about nature. Or should we? But what about us?

Model

In a circular particle accelerator, we have protons collide with protons in order to verify the existence of even smaller particles that are anticipated by theory. A new linear particle accelerator is currently in the planning stage. In it, electrons will collide with protons to enable supplemental precision measurements of mass and to advance the search for additional particles, such as the supersymmetric partners of the elementary particles. The goal is to understand the origins and development of our universe, and to decipher the laws that drive these processes, to the extent that such laws exist.

Microcosm, macrocosm, and in between them, we as researchers on the lookout. Findings concerning the state of science and technology only pass the test if there is relentless and unsparing criticism of the situation. Beyond that, we are not spared the ongoing process of weighing the risks of technical applications in keeping with the motto of "the technically feasible versus the economically and socially acceptable." For example, I read with astonishment about uncertainties in geo-engineering. Some scientists asked the Dalai Lama for advice on whether it would be acceptable to bring about global cooling by means of aerosol injections into the stratosphere.

Historian and cabaret performer Egon Friedell has repeatedly constructed parallels: The section on atomic fragmentation in "Gone to the Devil" of 1931 states: "The release of 'intra-atomic' energy would naturally result in a complete revolution of all earthly proportions. On the other hand, only the very naive could suppose that this would also signify a solution of the social problem. As the so-called 'normal person'–who is in fact not that at all, but the lord of our economic life– is born and dies an unimaginative knave, we may assume that such triumphs of technique would, like those that came before it, only lead to new forms of universal greed and injustice. One has only to imagine that two hundred years ago someone prophesied the extent to which humanity would succeed in utilizing magnetic energy, electric energy, solar energy, the energy in black coal, and the water energy that is stored up in 'white coal'– and what perfectly natural conclusions as to a social paradise the philanthropists would have drawn from it all! Instead, everything has become much worse, and Europe is divided into capitalist states wherein most people are beggars, and Soviet states wherein all of them are. No, by the 'activation of the atom' only the superiors would become even more greedy, the lower ones even poorer, so that both would become even more hungry and the wars even more brutal; ... The solution of the social problem calls for a moral emanation, ray-production, and atom-destruction."

Parallel Worlds

Democritus's deliberations from antiquity illustrate a comparison: the emergence of only one single cosmos within infinite space is just as improbable, he postulated, as one single stalk of grain growing alone in a large field. In the atomistic model and materialism of that time, there were countless atoms and endless space. The atoms are continuously in motion and they form in clusters that lead to the emergence of maelstroms and/or vortices, out of which worlds then form.

Around each world forms a membrane or covering made of atoms, with which it is delimited. The worlds are of different extents, and between them is empty space.

Plato disagreed with Democritus's atomistic principles insofar as he recognized only one world with one single creator. Later, however, he considered five worlds to be more correct, in line with his Platonic solids.

For Aristotle, a multiverse in which every world had an epicenter was out of the question. In the Middle Ages, it was disputed whether the uniqueness of the world and the nature of creation was an imperative or whether God could also create other worlds if He wanted to.

Aristotle's interpretation, which says the existence of more than one world is fundamentally impossible, was condemned by the church in 1277.

Giordano Bruno believed that in an unlimited universe existed a finite number of endless worlds, and that nothing existed outside of this universe.

Descartes refuted the existence of parallel worlds as follows: The nature of material lies solely in the fact that it is an expanded substance, which, he believed, must fill every space, thus also all possible spaces that other worlds might occupy. Consequently, there can be only one world.

Kant thought it made sense to assess the probability that parallel worlds exist if talking about spatially differing, non-three-dimensional universes. If we see the existing world as part of a multiverse, it would not be surprising that such a multiverse contains, among other things, other worlds that fulfill the complicated prerequisites that make human life possible. (Richard Dawkins)

By contrast, because of the logical impossibility of empirically measuring other worlds, the theory of multiple worlds is not a physical, but a metaphysical one and therefore on a par with the belief in a God the Creator, which is in comparison "more elegant and economic." (John Polkinghorne)

This subject and the theories and hypotheses associated with it thus appear to be like a fish: Something is built up, collapses, then slips away and vanishes. A Fata Morgana Ping-Pong.

The overlapping of theories only proves the existence of our overflowing power of imagination.

The butterfly effect spreads political isms, religiously motivated quarrels, peace through fear, East-West blocs, slogans, stereotypes of the enemy, an endless number of ideas, and eternal pressure to believe in the multiverse of individualities.

A parallel society is, per definition, a self-organized minority that has come into being as the outcome of a collision of interests. Although, of course, the social relevance of race and gender is always forgotten; the theater of separate worlds is in a constant struggle for power. Furthermore, a parallel world describes psychological patterns of behavior that are symptomatic of escapism. With fantasy, we can live out desires, wishes, or needs in our heads, or suppress unbearable circumstances. Viewed in a positive light, our imagination thus brings us regeneration and relaxation like in a dream.

A masterful further development is instrumentalization of faith, in order to create the ability to lucratively and effectively benefit from the notion of parallel worlds. From trading in indulgences to renunciation to warmongering bolstered by suicide attackers full of ideals, the afterlife is conjured up as a place of retribution. This parallel world is so effective and sinister that, right in the midst of our supposedly rationally enlightened, peace-loving world the bombs explode ... the torn-apart idealists will wonder all the more on the other side.

The chief technology officer of Cisco says, "The future will be about sensors and the Internet of Things, and how they will start influencing what we do." So here we have the idea that "technology will become an extension of who we are as human beings," and the notion that we will likely "inject a lot of sensors that will keep track of what's happening in our bodies, so it can be much more predictive ..." et cetera. The talk is of we, even though it's actually about the human body. The boundaries are blurred.

Google, too, is investing in this human-machine future, expending as much as the national budget of a medium-sized industrialized country, with the aim of creating the first mutant of an independent generation by 2045—very definitely a parallel universe.

Zuckerberg's Facebook do-gooder idyll stands before the ruins of its own idea. The parallel world this engenders is reality, and of course it wants to assert itself and blare everything out in order to secure the truthfulness of its existence via fake news.

These chain reactions of communications appearing on a massive scale require a suitable sensor system and appropriate navigation. Perhaps we will, in a certain sense, experience this technology like the blossoming of the agave.

Fantasy

The intergalactic conscientious objector is confronted with the following question, asked by the Interstellar Commission: "What would you do if bloodthirsty hordes from other planets attack us, try to read our minds, rape our women, and kill our children?" In response, the intergalactic conscientious objector says, in a relaxed tone: "If they think like us, it won't come to that." The commission withdraws to discuss the matter, and gives no answer. Not until much later does a letter arrive, transmitted telepathically: intergalactic conscientious objectors are not wanted on planets in habitable zones.

Money makes the world go round. Money behaves like a drop of water in relation to the nearest puddle: it accumulates, becoming ever more. It becomes a vast ocean, and in line with the advice of Baltasar Gracián to "disdain what you cannot achieve!" our hero decides on the motto "money is no object." After all, what role should it play if he has none anyway and has taken the path of contempt?

The squaring of the circle: the belief in a goal at the end of the path, the belief in a good and just society, is disappearing. The irony of the narrative: The individual has the feeling of being superfluous while at the same time, the biological sciences are hard at work on immortality. (Zygmunt Bauman) The essence of intelligence relevant to the development of technology is to analyze a situation in order to deduce what will happen in the future. Thus, artificial intelligence is defined and promoted in abridged form.

Flight

Regrettably, there is a well-founded suspicion that disparate fantasies born of thoughts of escape are promoted in art and culture, and that as a result, too much creative energy is misguided and misappropriated: houses that hang ultra-high on geostationary asteroids to solve artificial problems in expensive places, for example, or the colonization of other planets.

When all positive creators sink into abstract dreams of escape and thoughts of mammon, we relinquish the elaboration of the future to the obtuse.

The rapid technological transformation must not be allowed to trigger an escape into either a bland Biedermeier or a premature ossification in wisdom. We have to find and establish an appropriate framework of conditions. Bill Gates says: "When people are afraid of progress instead of delighting in it, we have a real problem."

We

We are not here, but exist as an external effect—each and every one of us.

Kindly forgive my sweeping arc of thought, a measured self-overestimation in recognition of the modest means of comprehension.

Still, it is needed so as to point out to the We, in which every human being plays a role, the immense importance of actions between me and you in the face of the impending isolation.

We should enlighten our minds in order to slow down the warming up of our mother ship, and think about what responsible-minded way of life we, each in our own way as imaginative beings, can contribute to the society.

Our potential: Seven billion people, and no one is the same the other. Except for doppelgängers. Georg Driendl

7

Anthropocene

We've made it. Our Mother Earth is at her wits' end with us. We've taken over the helm. At present it's not quite clear yet how we want to navigate onward, but one thing is already certain: we're doing it. This moment of takeover, when we assume control for nature, has been looming for some time now. But it was not known whether nature might be available as a copilot after all. Regrettably, we must rule out the vision that nature will be available to us afterwards; we can have no illusions about that. Only our fertile imagination, trained through multiple suffered experiences, gives us hope that, just as in all previous occasions of darkness that have been committed to memory and genetically stored, a way out can be found at the last second. In the end, that will leave the planet cold.

history

people are the fastest when it comes to prejudice
and the most forgetful when it come to their own history

Pottendorf.
Häus In

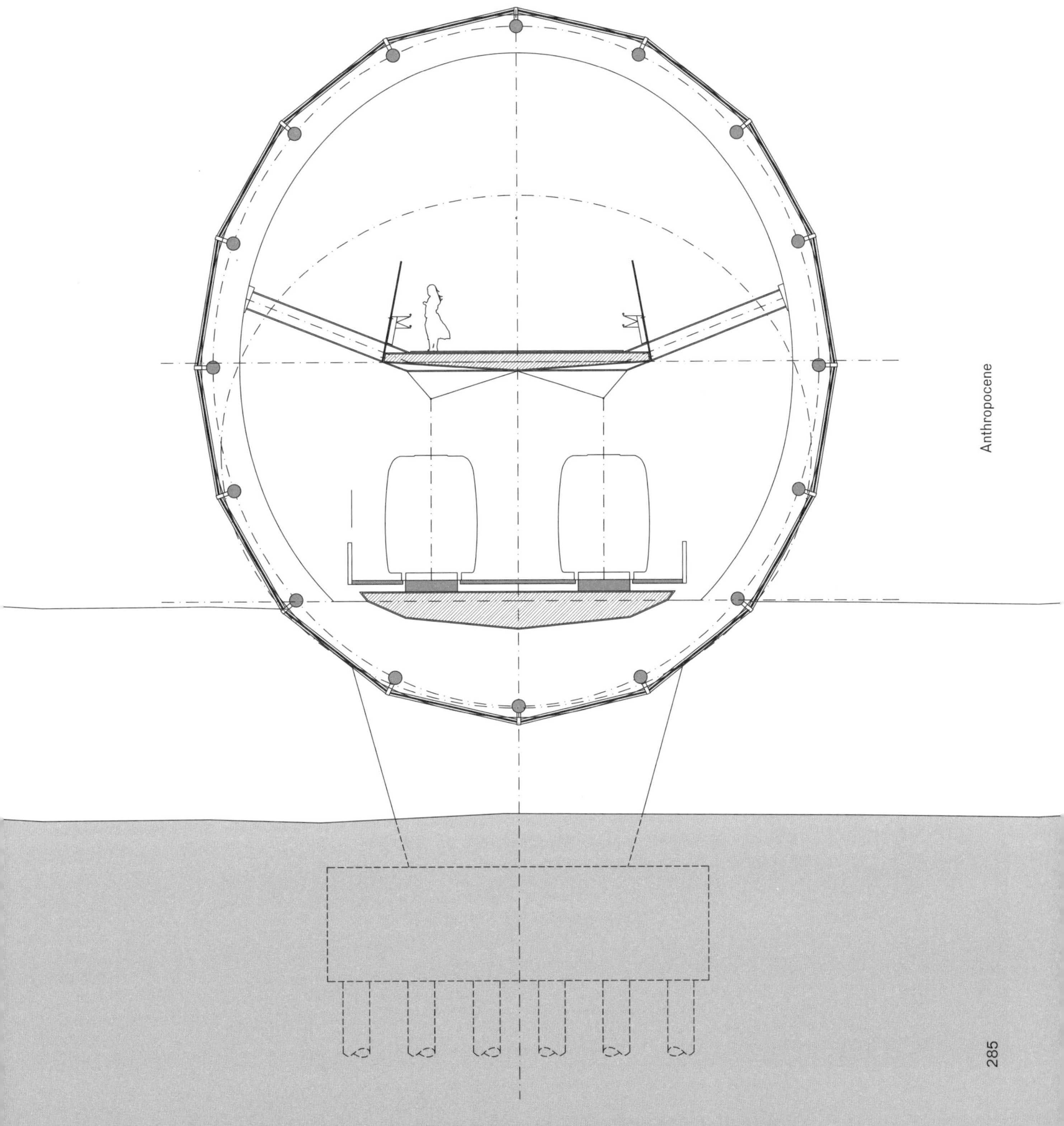

understanding is hard
being understood is easy
understanding understanding is hard
having understood is easy
not wanting to understand is easy
tolerating not understanding is hard
supporting understanding is easy
not tolerating is hard

sensing is easy
feeling is hard
letting yourself go is easy
letting someone go is hard

the good go into the mind
the many into the pot
the bad ones I want not
and you?

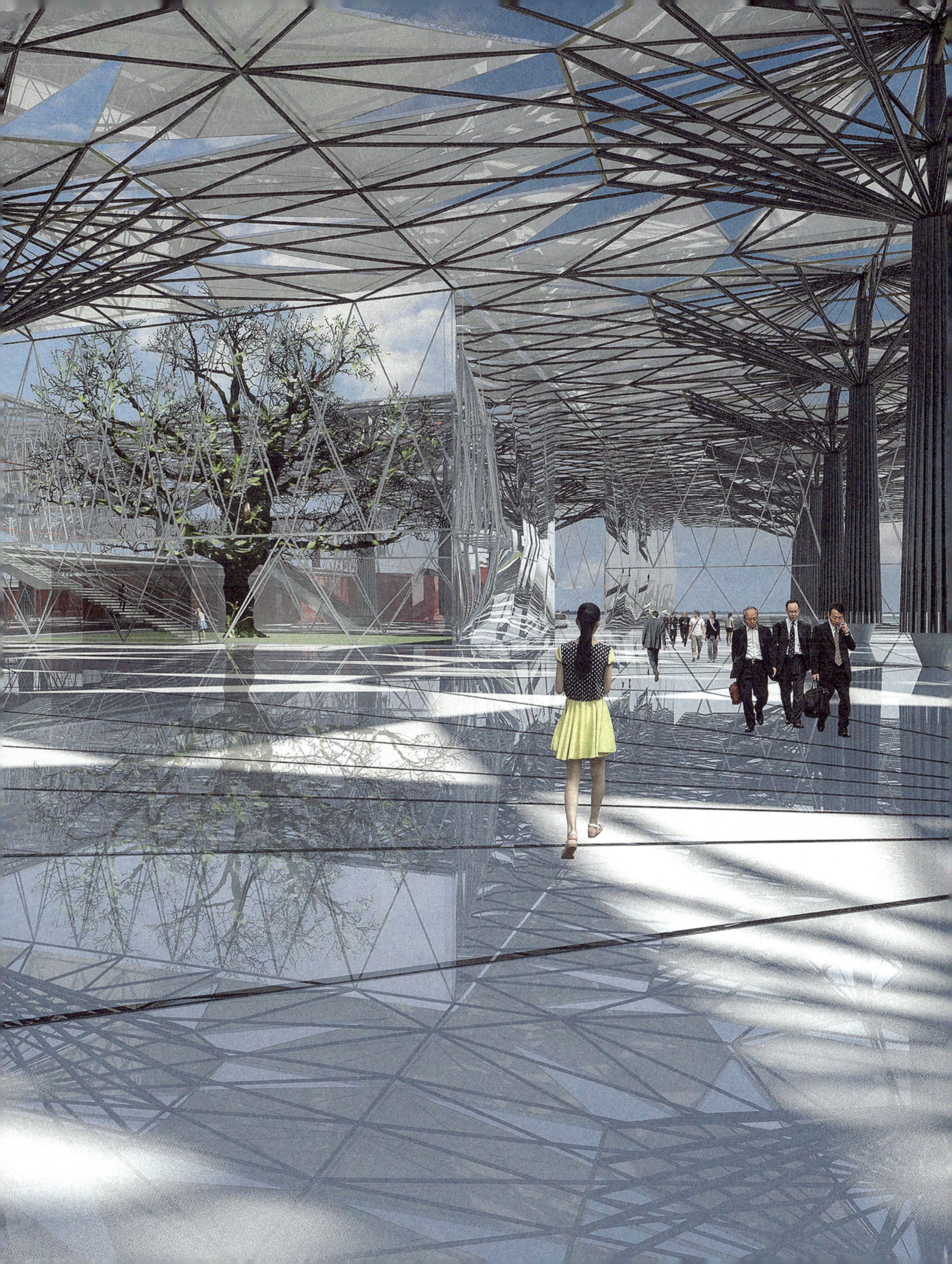

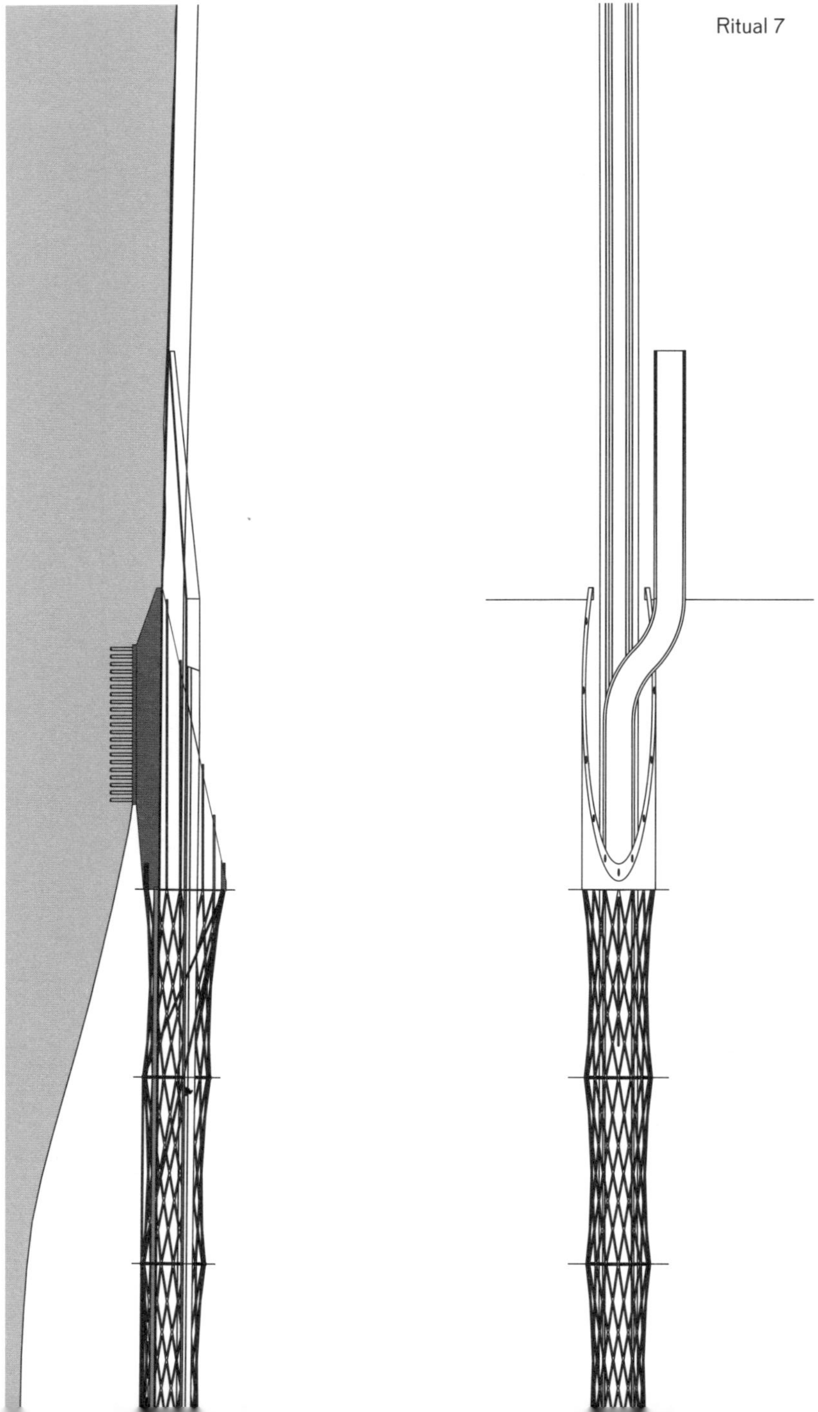

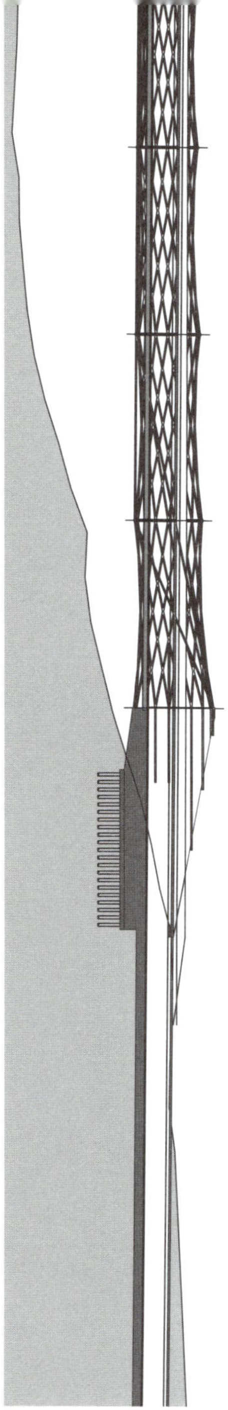
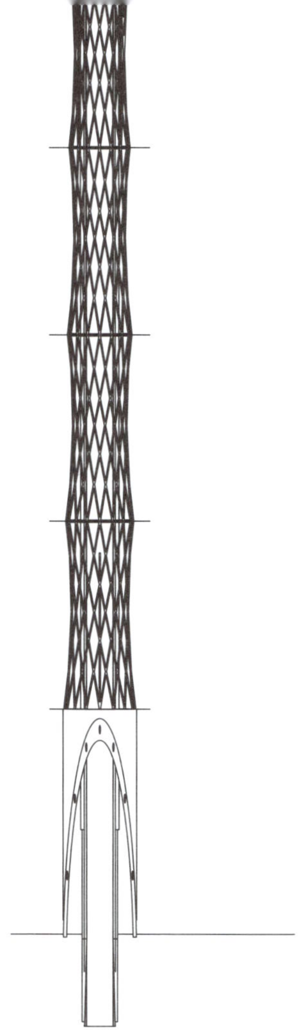

we are the polis
the theme is the role
every person is different
influenced
reared
left alone
intellectual
friendly
et cetera
distinguishing between people expresses a will against all
live, love, and celebrate differences
we are the polis
I am the will
similar is manymuch
equal is nothing

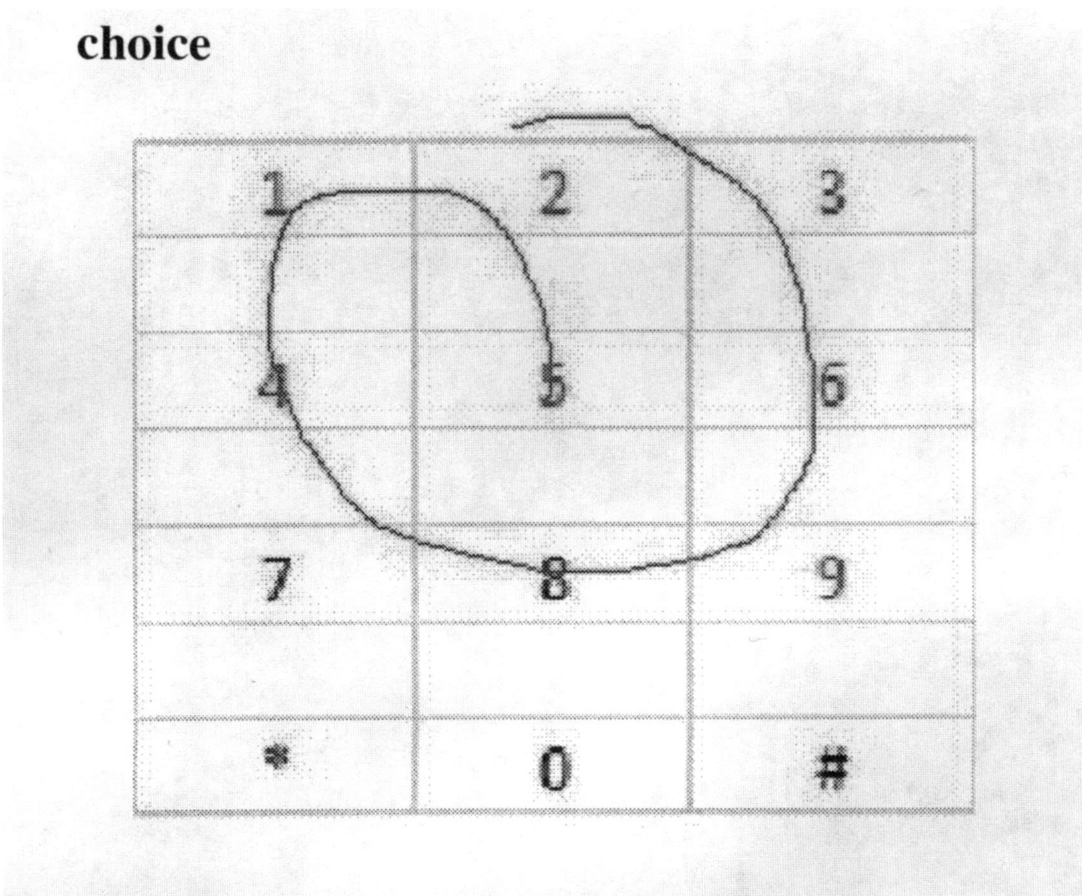

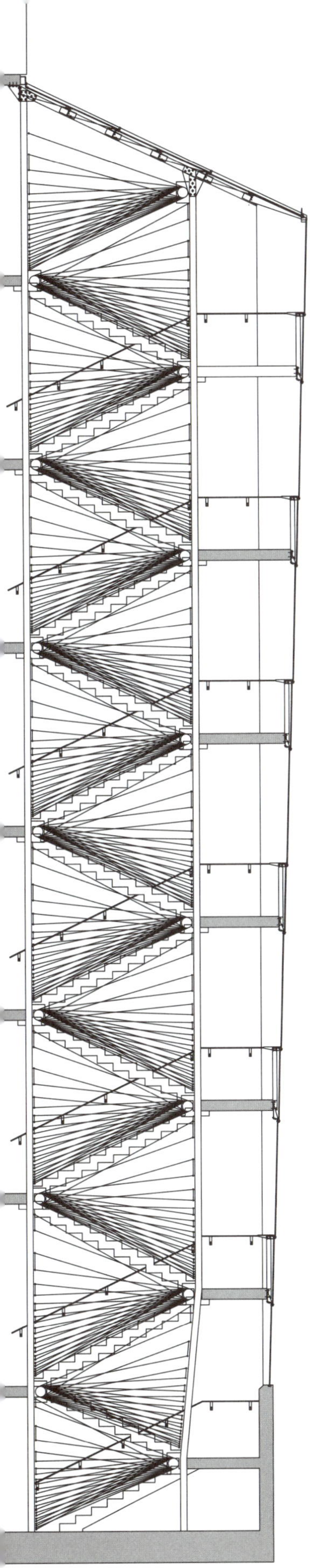

but

but go
but this
but also
but please
but when
but look
but why
but not
but because
but they
but thus
but say
but today
but the people
but quickly
but so what
but good
but me
but since
but
never

I

I spent my childhood in a village, lying on a sunny terrace and surrounded by mountains. Our house is situated in the middle of a small community at a fork in the main street leading to the church. My grandfather was a wainwright, blacksmith and carpenter, my grandmother a singer. My father struggled with an injury he had sustained in his youth. It had forced him to end his schooling; they had wanted to amputate his leg. My mother came from a region that was considered to be far away back then, close to the Swiss border. My grandmother told us children stories, and each year, guests from England showed the movies from their visit the previous year.

I really wanted to have a brother, and this wish was soon fulfilled.

The local elementary school was only a few houses away. I had a likable teacher in the first two years but an overly pedantic one in the third and fourth grades, and an extremely belligerent priest tended to our spiritual needs. In springtime, our main occupation was spying on the neighbors' gardens, waiting impatiently for the best fruits to ripen, but their consumption often ended in tummy aches and extended visits to the toilet. With my grandfather's help, I built a peculiar toy of my own design. The teachers encouraged us to draw and paint, which developed into my first source of income as our wealthy aunt routinely made acquisitions when she came to visit, with our grandfather acting as the gallerist. Our parents ran a general store that sold an extensive range of goods. The idea was to make sure that everything the village residents and their guests needed was in stock at all times. This meant, for example, that we carried all the available international daily newspapers, and at the end of each week, my grandfather and I then spent fascinating hours sorting those remaining for their return. While we sat there sorting, he told me lots of stories about his life, and we often lost ourselves in one or the other interesting article. I still clearly remember a statement he made at the beginning of the 1960s, that "the future belongs to the computer."

On the last day of school, the principal came into the classroom and pointed at me and my friend. Oh no, what had we done wrong? But when he said, "You two are going to Innsbruck, to the next-higher school," the whole class burst into laughter. A decision had to be made: either attend an academic secondary school as a boarding student far from home, or a general secondary school and ride the bus every day. I became a commuter. That meant a whole new set of challenges for me—getting up early, enduring bus rides that quickly became boring, helplessly putting up with the silence or questions of whoever was sitting next to me, and the constrained feeling of being wedged together like sardines in a can. It soon became apparent that the 35- to 50-minute morning bus ride was, of course, too short and too bumpy to do my homework. The buses didn't run that often, so if I missed mine, the school had to be informed of my absence, "due to illness."

In my free time I pursued my favorite activity: building things. Trained in handicrafts by our grandfather, following his instructions and using his tools (admittedly he was not always aware of it), we children built tree houses, huts, dams and even underground tunnels. The occasional passer-by must have wondered about the strange goings-on in the woods.

At the end of the fourth year in middle school, at which point I had broken the school record for absenteeism due to my intense extracurricular activities, there was, as was usual back then, career counseling. Scared that I might be given poor advice, I simply informed my parents that the advice I received was to attend the federal higher technical school in Innsbruck. My father did not oppose the idea, as he had started off there himself.

I passed the entrance exam and was set go to the technical college. From the very beginning, drawing was taught at a professional level; we learned freehand and tracing, sketching, descriptive geometry, architectural drafting, devising construction details—it was just what I wanted to do. I immediately recognized that drawing could bring me closer to "real" building.

People back home were pleased; my parents were happy and told everyone about their son at the technical school. The school occupied nearly all my time, 43 hours a week plus travel time. I increasingly lost contact with my friends in the village; we only met every now and then, on special occasions. An intense competition presided over the school, inflamed by the policies of some of the teachers. "At most only half of you will manage to pass the course, so the others had rather start an apprenticeship right away to make way for the others." The result was an almost unbearable overzealousness. My saving grace was that I loved what I was doing. One day, this positive feeling was interrupted as one of the instructors asked the class: "Who here wants to become an architect?" Only one person raised his hand—needless to say, it was me—and the class burst out laughing. How embarrassing.

Around this time my grandfather died. He emerged from his room walking upright without assistance, went past us with a "Pfiat Gott"—which translates as "God bless you"—got into the waiting ambulance and left us forever. His last wish—to live longer than our grandmother, who was dependent on the care of another—did not come true. From that point on, my mother took care of her until, one day, my grandmother called all the family members to her side to take her leave. Her words to me were, "Georg, you have to go out and learn a lot, a whole lot!" She refused to acknowledge two of her daughters, reiterating her conviction benignly, and not even the well-intentioned intervention of my mother could change her mind. The two daughters had not visited their ailing mother in all the preceding time. After each of us had seen her, she passed away. The battle that subsequently broke out within the family over her inheritance was a terrible time for my parents, my brother and me.

As I was doing so well at college, I was soon able to carry out some building plans in the village. A small house, an addition and a breakfast room yielded just enough money for me to buy an old car. I was no longer a student riding a bus, now I was a student who drives his own car.

At the graduation ceremony, my class teacher recommended that I go to Vienna to study architecture. That seemed familiar to me! My parents supported the proposition, but that was tempered with regret at not being able to give me any financial support to get started. I applied to take the entrance exam for the Academy of Fine Arts and was accepted into one of the two master classes for architecture. While I was not a stranger to the urban fabric of a town, this was a big city and there was no escape. Thanks to my training, I had no problem finding work. I was only seldom able to make trips to visit my family while studying, as I spent semester breaks working. I had contact with lots of people, something was always going on somewhere, but real friends were few. I met my future wife toward the end of my studies. She brought her two-year-old daughter with her and it was love at first sight. Our son was born shortly after and our new family evolved into a safe haven in a storm. I now had to finish my studies quickly, and that meant working less and studying more. Because my parents and my wife supported me in this with every effort possible, I soon attained my degree, and was also awarded top honors with the "Meisterschulpreis." I was finally one step closer to turning my passion into my profession. After some theoretical deliberations on the subject of architecture and my first practical experience as an employee working for some of my colleagues, I set up my own office. I soon discovered that building only makes sense when you do it with and for other people. To this day, the essential challenge remains unchanged: expanding one's horizons and staking out a position in relation to society. The work begins, of course, with the idea on paper, but then other people come into play—otherwise what you have envisioned in your mind simply remains on paper. The statement "architecture is a job for old men" (Hans Hollein) now has tangible meaning for me. When you manage to turn an idea into reality by working together with others, and you can see that what you conceived, planned and built now delights others, then you have done your job right. That is the reward of being an architect.

Today, my wife, my daughter and my son all work together with me in our studio. When possible we also try, through internal cross-financing and the cultivation of friendships and cultural contacts, to work across geographic borders.

A well-known, quite notorious Viennese barkeeper, who helped by drowning the occasional worry or pleasure in alcohol-infused philosophy, once asked me out of the blue and at a very late hour, “Tell me, do you have a friend?” When I hesitated with my reply, he became more vehement, adding, “You don’t have a friend, there’s no friend anymore.” I said no and insisted he was wrong, but at the same time, it became clear to me that he might just be right. This unpleasant realization had a sobering effect, and I answered with conviction: “I have a friend.” His response came as no surprise, saying: “Then prove it, call him and ask him to come over, because if he’s your friend, he’ll come.”

I called my friend, and he came, and he is still my friend today. The barkeeper and the other guests couldn’t believe their eyes. That was 15 years ago.

We. Georg Driendl

8

Paradise

Paradise is the state we would be in if it weren't for our guilty conscience. It pinches here and there, sometimes more and sometimes less. A chronic subliminal plague of losing something that doesn't even belong to you, and never will. Why even live in New York or talk to the animals in the jungle? Just recalling the famous, eternally boring state immediately triggers a violent reaction. People act as if remote-controlled, driven by a nagging conscience to force a slight change without bringing about any special recognition of the familiar situation. Every outbreak tears a hole in the world. Time and again, even in the dynamics of the group—and indeed on a massive scale—greed creeps in, multiplied by lightning-fast attacks on everything valuable.

LODOMERIA

love a
nothing can I give you
all that is mine is also thine
nothing is enough
all is too little
nothing in motion
all is dancing
nothing whistles the wind
all falls silent
nothing on top of each other
all is scattered
nothing without value
all is just here
nothing left alone
all with you
g

airtight poem

new program
architecture without air pollution
…
building material air
1966
2016
after 50 years of proclamation
status quo
copyright expired
a happy year
air
hot air
moist air
heavy air
thin air
dry air
cold air
…
matter is displaced air
architecture of air
aerostatics
trapped air
air-filled tires
aerodynamics
motion is airshipment
everywhere air
airless outer space
airspace
and in between, matter
…
the displacement of air by matter is architecture
dynamic thanks to motion
statically encapsulated and upholstered
chemically burned
respiration
…
cushion of air
air pillow
a tire
air pressure
comfortably suspended ride
air in motion is wind
stagnant air
sticky air
no air
…
light as a feather we escape gravity

loophole for sunshine

when it goes, when it comes, wind and weather
and sunshine
the heart does not complain, it beats on
but faster
it's so small
and yet it finds
a loophole
for the warmth to shine

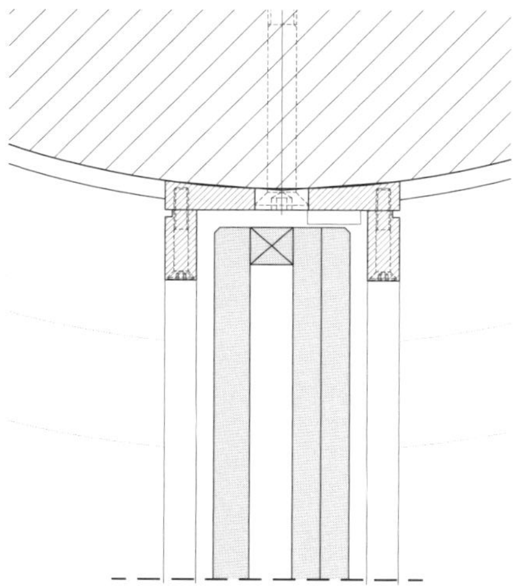

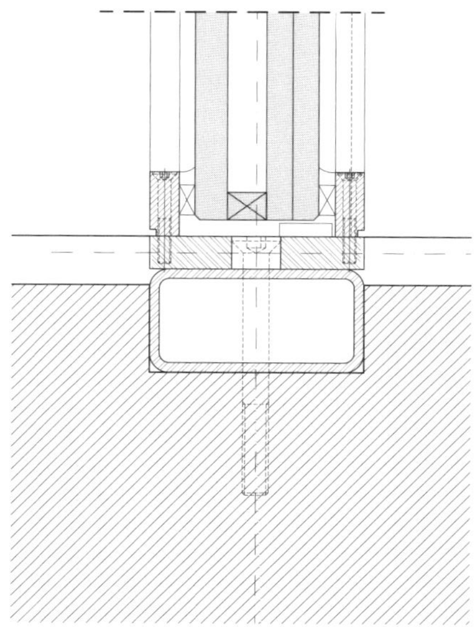

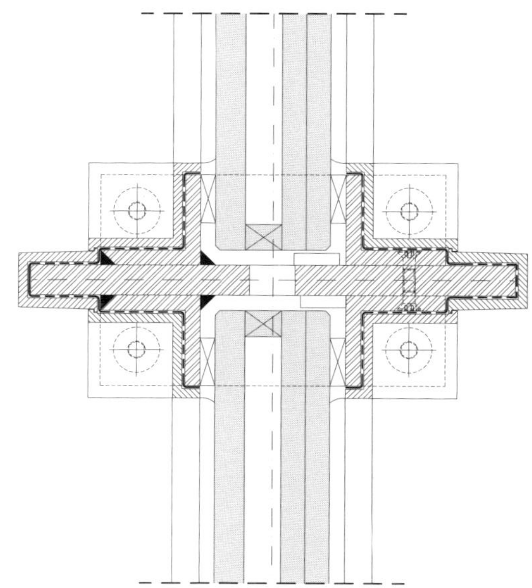

Like the protective leaves of flowers in bud, 3 polytetragonal bodies envelop a cube of clearly defined geometric form that is not visible at first from the outside. The borders and points of contact of these bodies allow the inside to flash outward at the edges. Light and the surroundings are thus integrated. These "fissures" along the edges, between the opaque bodies, are a source of daylight inside. Once through the portal, you move from the forecourt across the diagonal of the square at the base to enter the chapel. The space symbolizes gender equality on multiple levels: left half, right half, the relief of the interior walls as raised and recessed, vertical / horizontal - at 2:30 pm a ray of sunlight cuts through and unifies the cube.

The load-bearing, formative basis of the chapel is the fourth body, which, linked to the mass of the forecourt, floats above the water. The atmosphere inside this chamber of luminous resonance is light and cheerful; it's kept a secret from outside and only revealed upon entering - "hidden squareness" in the midst of nature.

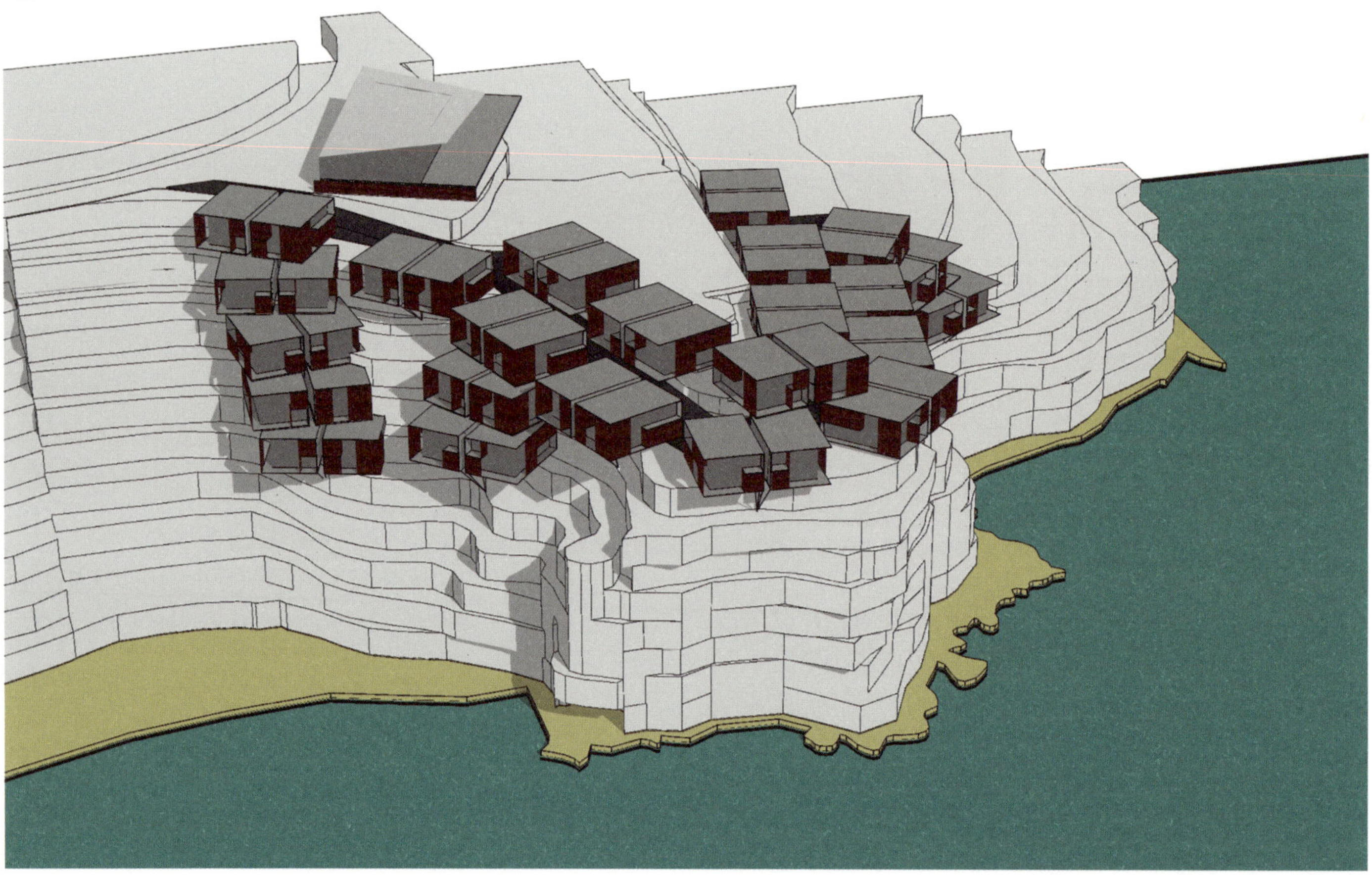

hand on heart
hand on your heart on hand
tomorrow without frills

The Countryside in the City

unfetter
wild
now

Greed has obviously set off a chain reaction. The decision. The best piece of the pie cannot be left to chance. No. It must of course be allocated to someone. But to whom? You're still asking that? To us, of course.

My dear Sir, it's up to you; you have to decide. Or are you the indecisive type? Indecisive people should leave the decision-making to us. We behind the scenes naturally know exactly what decisions should be made, as well as how and when. Decisions are very important. If necessary, the arguments for them can be delivered later, but first of all a decision must be reached about what is to be said by whom, about how to proceed and in what direction, and about whom to trust. We immediately sense the harmony when someone takes control, then we feel very secure, especially when it comes to our agendas. We would like you to have this feeling of security when everything is under control. Now. Nobody has made any demands yet, but if we don't decide immediately, everyone else will say what they want. Then we'll be in a jam. Everything and nothing. Everybody adds their two cents, whether or not they've been asked and whether or not they're involved. Originator? What's that? Are we not all in the position of originators, or of those who assert claims to copyrights? My originator is a nice woman; I'll ask her where she comes from. If she answers, "I don't know," in that very second, I'll feel like she is deceiving me. Why?

A Blistering Afterthought

With the reins in your control and forced into a corner, you have two options: either give up or attack head-on—the element of surprise, the heroic saga.

Speaking from the center: How does that which we call architecture come about? An environment that constantly renews itself, either slowly or more quickly, showing either more caution or more brutality in dealing with that which has developed over time. Tabula rasa. New and germ-free—besides all the garbage, of course. Those who are not settled have never had any time to imagine life within a traditional, stationary, and permanent shell. They are always on the move, up and away, having wiped away the traces. Those who are settled live their lives in a stationary and stable shell. This notion is defended statically; the erosion is held at bay. The juxtaposition of these diametrically opposed ideas is more or less the foundation upon which our modern city is built. This image is a composition formed by very many individual decisions, singular actors, and very different interests, all of which crowd into the center. The surrounding countryside is magnetized and sucked in. The magnetic, the heroic saga, the melody of inexhaustible opportunities. The perspective congeals to become the source of constant renewal and change. The city pulsates and develops into a monstrous whole made up of individual desires that can obviously never be satisfied in full. The edges of our metropolises are completely out of control. Everyone seems paralyzed by the glamour of the center, and it is precisely here that architecture comes into play as a stylistic device of what seems to be expected.

Architecture Is

Architecture is a huge parvenu that one can pleasurably lean on in order to say: Look! We have shown the world again. How imposing something inherently rigid and unchanging can appear so as to tell, again and again, the story of the changes that have occurred to the places where we have built, and, as a sign of our approval, to smuggle in this story sublimely—commensurate with the grandeur of the object itself—as a self-enhancing means of glorification among the flood of images. Seen from the perspective of the built object, burdened by the aura of epochal significance, we fail—amid the spectacle of silent fresh existence—to neglect the level of the orchestrated masses who have been groomed to expect a characteristic style. It is in the nature of things, when nothing exists except for the plan from before, to create something of epochal significance to galvanize all available forces and means, which then allow the design to be translated into the buildable, even if unusual processes are needed to do so. The goal is not to take an objective—no matter how large and complex it may be—and interpret it in the usual style of the times. Rather, the idea is to tell a story that merits gathering all the burdens together in order to give impetus to an energetic force and, in so doing, extract the built object from its silent role as an extra among many on set and imbue it with a soul. Only so can it be lively.

But

The fear of being naked screams for culture, and this drapes us in a coverlet of education that does not make it possible for us to implement direct action with mere words. Silent. Deaf. Terrified that something naked might appear. Exposed and at the same time shameless. Only in this condition, naked, do we recognize our helplessness in these turbulent times. Our vulnerability is the thin fragility of our skin. Its suitability seems to have been lost over the millennia through the routine practice of covering ourselves up. We plunge from one adventure to the next, always on the run. Always on the lookout for originality, again and again. Our thin skin, and atop it a second and a third layer in which, without worry, we move, speak, dance, sing, laugh, eat, sleep, love, and make war—only to then do it all over again from the very beginning. Are you saying that carrying all that baggage doesn't change us? Going from nakedness to being covered up, from birth onward. Any other condition is unknown; everything is veiled, and every communication must first penetrate the shell, like an icebreaker in Arctic waters. Imposed upon ourselves, we are forced to demand of language that it have the penetrating power and explosive force of an anti-tank grenade that can pierce the shell. The program of sheathing ourselves runs in unison with the torpedoing through the weapon of speech. Our shell is becoming more impenetrable, our speech more aggressive. Babylon, all that simultaneous palaver; nobody understands anything anymore. Everyone is working on building a tower that will never be completed. This act of building is an ancient primal instinct that cannot be turned off. The slightest occasion and ... perhaps the drift of gravitation is the driving force. That just might be. That would explain the unexplainable. Likewise, that could also define the archaic notion of a canon that must be reinvented over and over.

The only things that are free and radical are our thoughts. One must, however, consider the sheer mass of thoughts that are thought worldwide. They convey only one message: to survive, naked and with no canon. Even research into our past history and our yet unseen future will hardly allow another outcome to manifest itself. In this context and at precisely this time, we should see what it means to build something while keeping a focus on the perspective of subsequent erosion. As the saying goes, time heals all wounds, but similarly, time also brings all the unexpected wonders. Time is not to blame and it also doesn't interfere, even when it is crookedly delayed. The only ones who can interfere are the clairvoyants, who can instill ideas in their contemporaries with their visions. This is taught to us by history, which designs the development of our becoming ever more profoundly. I'm not sure, but I cannot identify an obligatory path from the hand axe to the drone, or from the cave painting to the Internet, or from the wheel to the Tesla.

The obligatory path of what is still becoming, taking into consideration our growing mass of thought, is by comparison extremely calming.

And

Fear of change initially causes lethargy. Nevertheless, curiosity continuously drives us to the edge. Our expanded field of view over that which we have accumulated and captured propels us into outer space—beyond the atmosphere, to the exoplanets—and simultaneously into inner space—through the skin, to the freely available and inexhaustible, highly toxic, and immense energies in the tiniest speck of dust. An endless expanse of all dimensions, everything in motion: visible, audible, and direct. Along both routes we pass through multiverses on the lookout for our origins and the law, the philosopher's stone. We withstand the aggregate state of constant and rapid change by adhering in fear to a culturally determined illusion of an invariably flourishing, carefree life—a moment of the beautiful, the orderly, and the peaceful. Paradise, "the Garden of the Lord" (Persian). At this point, we can perhaps tether the manifestation of the term to a political function: Architecture is illusion or guiding vision. The illusion develops its impact as if it were reality, while the guiding vision develops its impact as reality. The illusion appeases, whereas the guiding vision empowers (and of course everything feasible exists in between). Take a few steps back and, through the fog, we see the Olympic discipline that was all about setting proportion, space, material and image in relation to context in a social ritual. It has nearly disappeared over the millennia, but reminiscence has embedded itself in our tradition of thought and has found a fixed place in our European social self-image. No lamentation, no criticism of petty things; everybody aims high anyway, even though almost no one actually achieves it. The top trends are transported into every living room via the Web; styles and fashions inevitably create a SENSATION at first. Or, secondly, they expose what was concealed, making it visible for freely perceived UNDERSTANDING. It goes without saying that a simple sensation is far more captivating than, by comparison, having to make an effort to understand something unpopular. To put it simply, something sensational is self-explanatory and requires no change whatsoever, while something with an instruction leaflet and a need for explanation must be repeatedly recreated. Thus, this is where the difference lies between the illusion and the guiding vision; high-performance and communications industries use this behavior intensely. Everyone wants to have a ritual piece of that pie; nobody wants to enter a cultural no-man's land. Everyone wants to jump on the bandwagon, knowing that not every vehicle actually reaches its destination, just because the chance to ride along occasionally arises. Nevertheless.

Movement is not scary; what scares us is being left behind alone. Moving, especially together with others, calms us and attracts magnetically. Progress brings everyone along.

Do you see the picture? If not, then form a picture of your own! And once again, there are two no-win endings in the corner: standstill or movement ahead. An exemplary visual culture.

Then

Is architecture created when enclosures are raised to the status of monuments?

Or: Architecture emerges when the site has become thoughtful!

The house, the bridge, the property, the village, the space, the special, the city, the established meeting point, the square, the urban canyon, the field of rubble, the urban landscape—and in between is open space, a lack of space, traffic, and crowding. At the corner is a crossing; its name is a form of remembrance. The material crumbles to small dusty particles, and this is how even the tiniest speck represents the will toward a monumental exaggeration of being.

The experts on quantum mechanics are invited to relativize this exaggeration. One day, in what might be almost the last speck of dust, we will have deciphered the genetic code of the very architect of a long-lost culture who once built paradise.

Architects are responsible for their fantasies—even if they are genetically programmed into their brainstems through tradition, transferal, or any other external influences, perhaps even by sorcery and quackery like tectonics, statics, or the spontaneously released physical force that propels us onwards.

Before that, however, we jump into our work vehicle and practice criticism of the system with an unimpeded view of bare wires!

From the building to the notion in general. Climatic cladding for low consumption, free of toxins. The plot.

The architecture of society—plus its development, technical and organic—onward to the city, to utopia and vision: the countryside in the city. From the previously modern—you could also say functional—to the romantically green, right up to today's utilitarian silence, silently astounded by the growth! A copied flexing of muscles sings along of wanting and the capriciousness of the possible. Below ground, in the water, on land, in the air, and even in space.

Back to the building! Now we understand; the post-Anthropocene shows effect. We'll change everything, concentrating on the cities and pulverizing the rest while we hyperventilate!

A new being takes form before our very eyes, outside the sphere of influence of our support—it drifts, prospers, and fevers in our imagination as a vision that spans from things we already know to a construct of that which we have yet to encounter. We celebrate the incessantly new, persecuted by its effects—run, run from it, run after it.

The conquest is suppressed. All over the world, cities develop identically, although their political systems are radically different. Capital nestles against the congealed surface. The community looks on, suspiciously benevolent. Dissemination is ensured.

Put on airs, do it differently, make yourself unrecognizable until you take flight, and of course, always do it all at once ...

Knowledge is our search for truth. If art lives, then it lives the right to lie. What attracts people to the city despite their latent fear of the new? In the city, everything is always new, even if it's a hand-me-down. The city is art. The city we seek is art, and free and wild. The city is our space of manifestation. The oscillating and vexing illusions of cities that continually reproduce themselves from within—growing, transforming, sprawling—are the daydream of a potent collective stimulant. To my mind, it is unnecessary to take history hostage or to hold it responsible; we are witnessing a metamorphosis, worldwide and up close.

The End?

"Is that where we are?" wonder those left behind by world architecture. Forgetfulness and performing services for the star cult cover up what it's really all about. If, quite simply, we are not talking about architecture as the creative output of a star, but as all that which is constantly being built—roads, power stations, airports, electricity grids and IT networks, switching systems, transport structures, Industry 4.0, et cetera—it immediately becomes clear that the mass of these infrastructures that span the globe have long since reached and even exceeded by far the volume of building work done in order to house people.

If all that is architecture, then we are not at the end but at the beginning.

The Chinese government's planning department is considering reopening the Silk Road, but this time under Chinese direction. And they are undoubtedly thinking as little about a renaissance of loam construction techniques as are the corporate groups from California's data empires.

As long as we continue to associate architecture with a dreamy, old-fashioned image of individual buildings that should follow a canon, regardless of the tradition, we are not speaking about architecture, but about a niche, closed off from its surroundings. The talk, disguised as discourse, attempts to separate niches from all the rest. What inevitably remains are then small closed circles, protected zones for a few protagonists. These small vortices within one eye of the cloverleaves of data highways are at best the justification for diverse outdated structures, whose interfaces are once again in the process of falling apart at the edges.

Neither the supposed end nor the detected smell of the new as it dawns upon us, perceived and scrupulously documented by the commentator, is the essence, but EVERYTHING else on the screen (route) is the architecture of the NOW. The picked-out detail is the grain of corn found by the blind chicken.

Admittedly, niche production at a massive scale could produce a pleasantly soothing breeze before the real storm reaches us. The sand in the eye of the hurricane will be carried along unnoticed.

Parallel paths, or how others and other things can be successfully hindered: The discovery of the cult genetic defect since 1945: ANSx45y. The defective gene leads to constant early detection with the goal of isolation and elimination of super talents. Discourse in the stew, thwart, there's nothing better coming along.

```
life
fixed in stone
under water
rooted in the land
urban tough
airy and free like a bird
pulse
```

Is architecture feminine? Architecture is feminine and free. End of the heroic sagas!

Who was it that came up with the idea of demanding something from society without ever having done anything to deserve it? What does it mean for society when someone engages with architecture? At this point we should bring to mind whether architects produce architecture quasi automatically, or whether architecture only makes sense in a social context, that is, it is only put to the test through its existence. Only when a requited love awakens the material with a kiss do we speak of architecture.

Anybody can make demands. Two meters to lie down, sit comfortably, move over, stand up and go.

An American fairy tale, the star cult versus the right to vote—this has been a paid advertisement! The incrustation of a thought calls for discipline and severity when dealing with the neurons beneath the skullcap.

Crosscheck

When a built object is used as a beacon for the questionably important, and thereby shrouds or alters its very own purpose, then what we have before us is a stillbirth. Opposed to this we have the monument, which reminds us of a specific event through the use of appropriate emblematics, clearly defined. The other thing is cladding that leaves such a dent in the underlying use that the function loses its primacy and the cladding itself becomes an autonomous object.

It is the expression of an extremely strange and pitiful will to dress an intended purpose in such a deformed manner that it is supposed to appear as a deliberately abstract and blurred message so as to deceive, through its lack of content, as a grand gesture and nonetheless be useful for tourism.

Rooster combs. Fluids become rigid. The archaic becomes modern. But always very expensive and above all big.

Built structures give us the opportunity to grant material form to wishes, fantasies, desires, and dreams, setting them in our path and rendering them as architecture; to invent travel destinations when the journey is for business purposes; to visualize belief and hope when we are required to thoughtlessly buy into the system; and to simulate progress if criticism should fail, so as to present a clear picture of the farcical blunder.

Good. We have these images; we need them, perhaps merely as a colonoscopy of our conviviality.

Simplifying caricatures help us to save the past in visual and enigmatic form, and thus the strenuous notion of a present is no longer necessary.

We are waiting in anticipation for the garrulous interpretations of the drifting of distorted time we can perceive of via the hearing organ of science.

The form, a straightforward result, is sold as a secret.

Now

What might our architecture and the architecture for our cities be? What makes it worth putting up with the hardship and the effort, worth leaving one's comfortable position to take up an operative position, working against old laws that blind us and values that bind us? Presumably we should not allow the art of experiencing to be taken from us. The distribution of the masses and energies is not controlled from outside. You know it. And even I know that this knowledge is founded on nothing. There is nothing in between. The city is art, architecture is life, and life is love. I have found nothing else. Georg Driendl

9

Now

Are we not fighting for the spiritual palaces of the republic? We human beings need the palaces—and in order to recognize the right ones, our soul must also be in the right place. Nothing new under the sun is now wrong. Omniscient and fully equipped, we find ourselves going down a one-way street; the consumer and the philosopher are both seeking reality. Science lays the foundations for the instruments; the gravitational waves have been measured. The readings enable us to listen deep within the empty, dark forest. The interpreter, now liberated from strained past and futuristic models as well as fashionably up-to-date ones, can again assemble something new and, if successful, concurrently interweave vision and reality, keeping everything in motion. It's now as easy as pie.

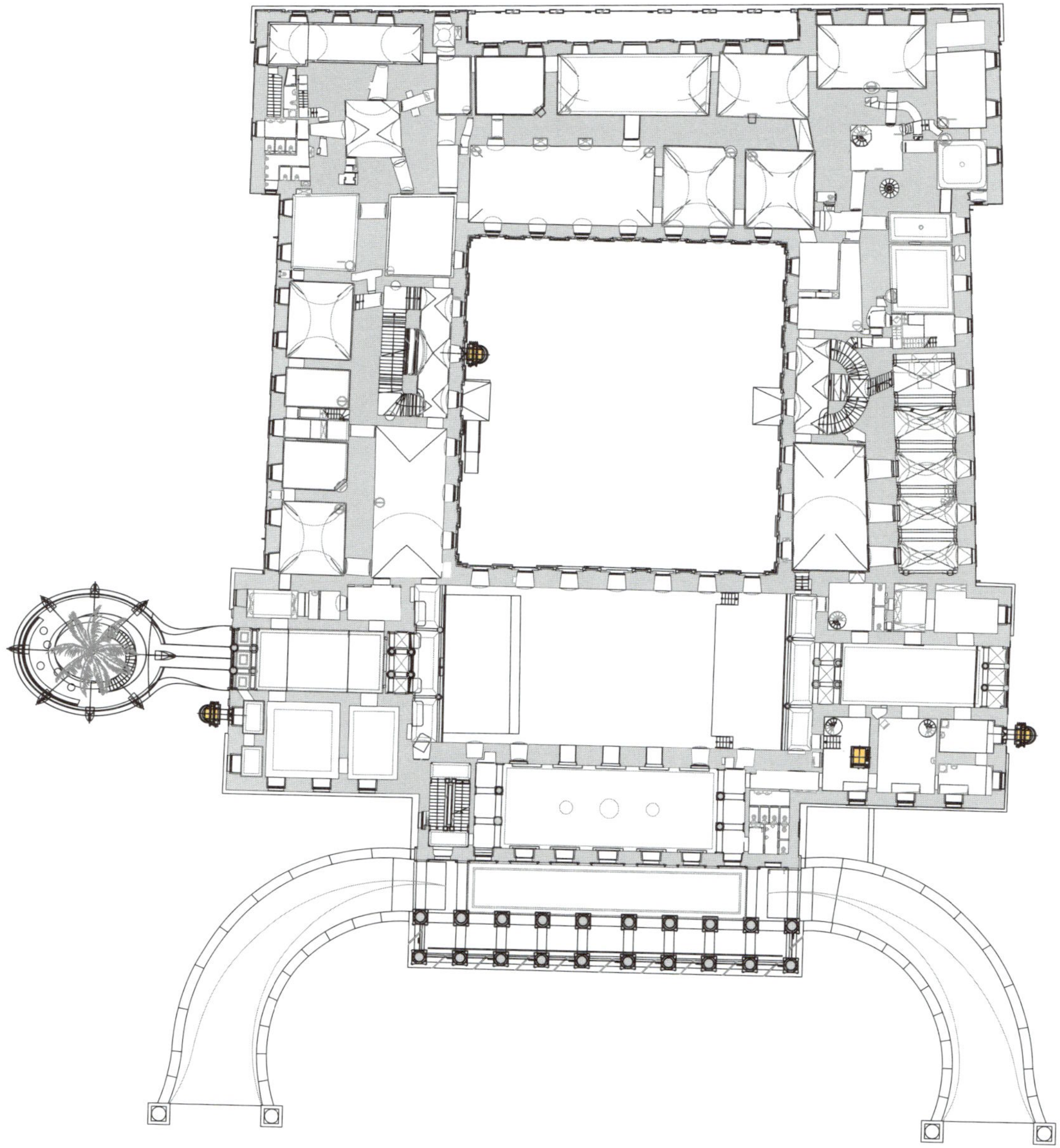

Now

interest
inter
est
disinter
est?
uninter es ting
ou

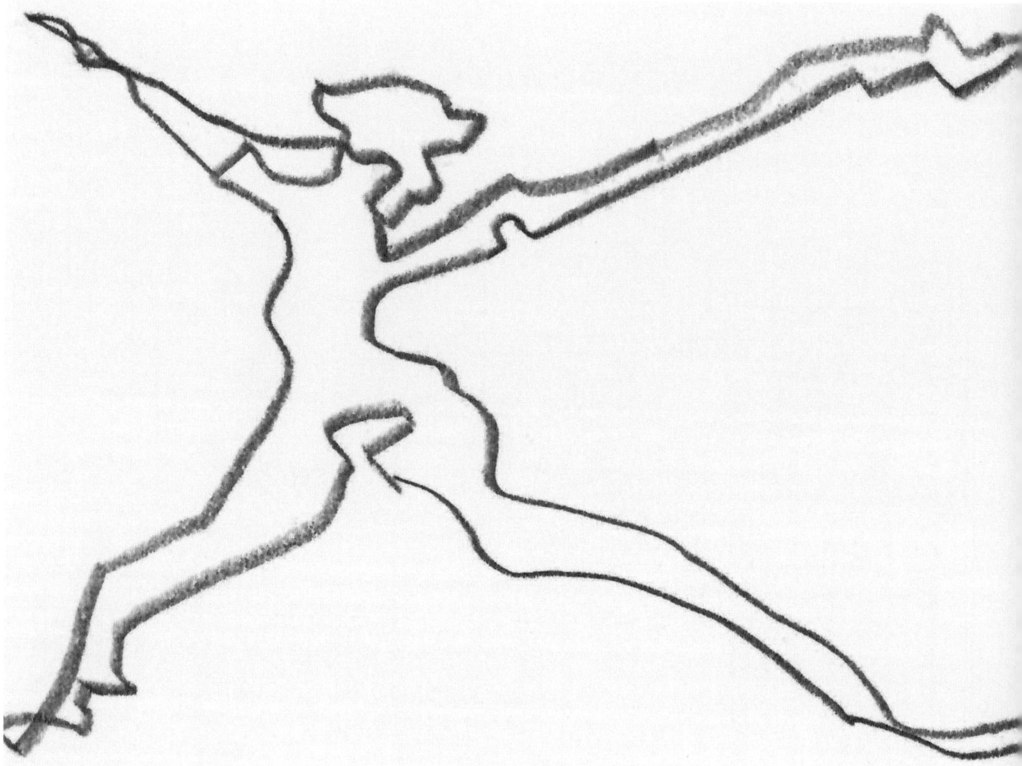

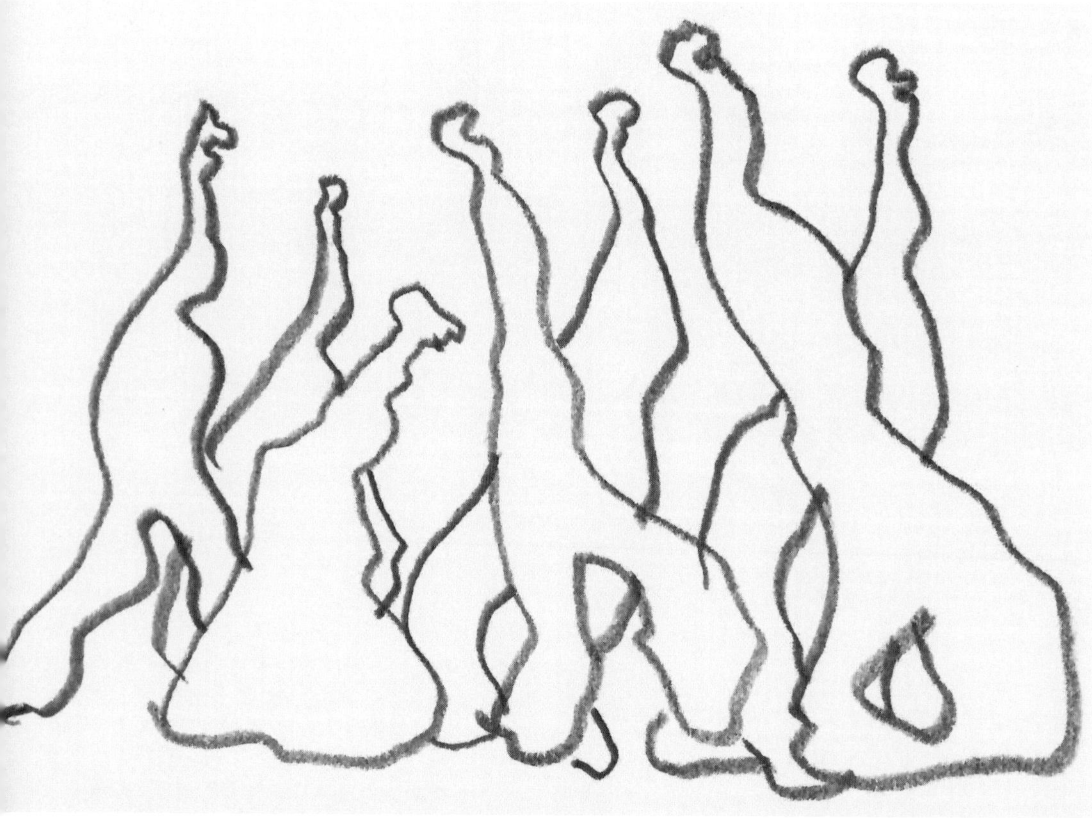

the american dream

new york dreams
the americans have their sights on mars
and ours are on nyc
the whole world wants the same
skyscrapers everywhere and
the western alternative
failed in '89
multicultural smart cityscape
we want all that too
vienna has donau city
riyadh has its financial district
and istanbul has maslak
everything chinese copied
hypertrophied
the egyptians had pyramids
we have nyc
the dream of glass
the dream of stone
the dream of sculpture
the dream of theory
the dream of complication

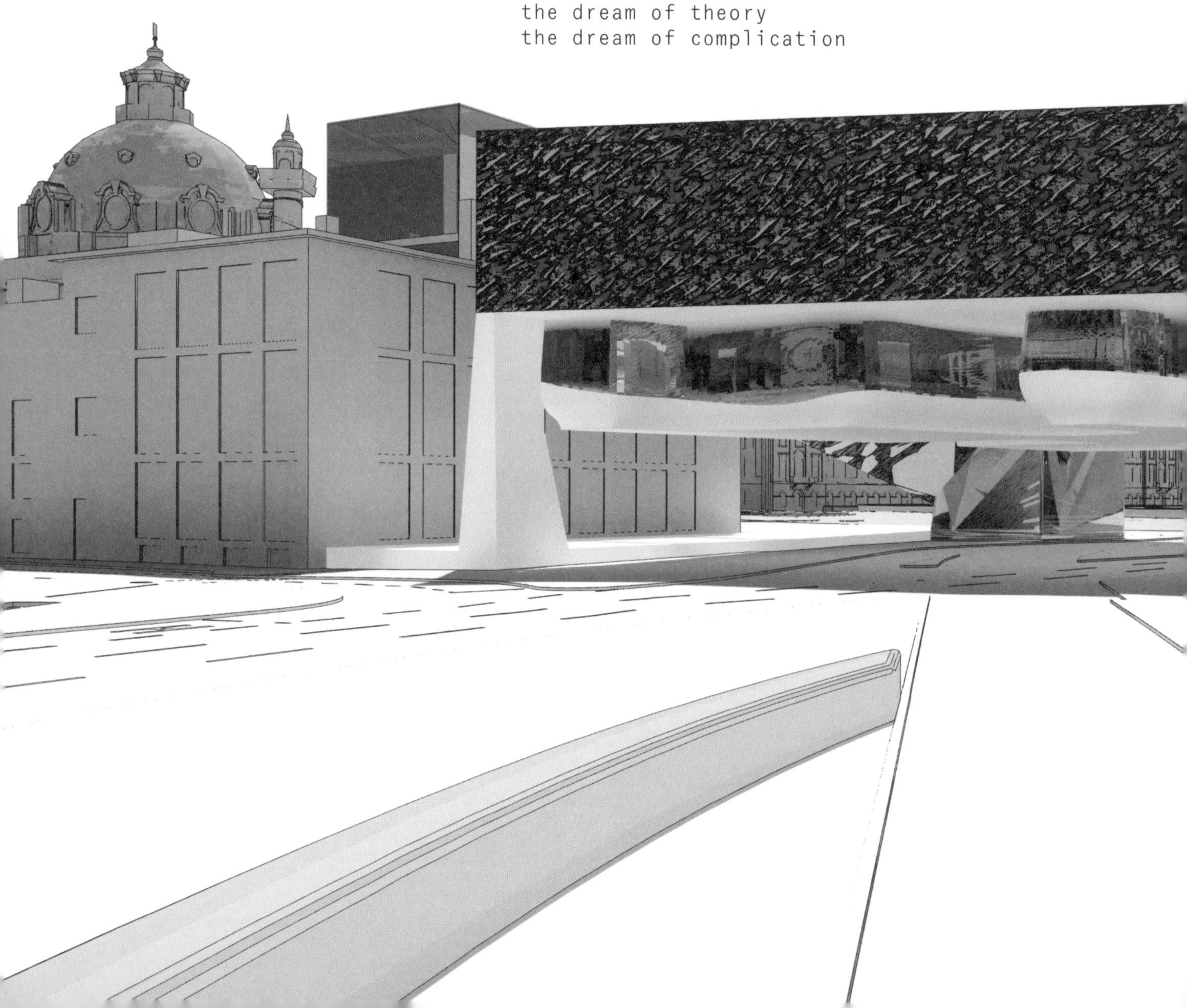

the tower
exported – not constructed
minimundus becomes a treasure trove
surreale irony
nyc is also without these dreams
nyc has no interest in these dreams
it is like it is
a dream
maybe a nightmare alp
all over concepts
1968 generation
super-stringent reference intelligence
generates air and plastic bubbles
nyc remains aloof
some greening perhaps
tomatoes on the roof
vertical plant breeding
self-sufficient
the highline for nearby recreation
employees effective for the financial industry
in the tightest of quarters, side by side
the dark canyon
finally
the cliff, the skyscraper, the corporation
is google's flagship store missing from manhattan?
the user's voice
google buys central park
most valuable place throughout the world
if the spider goes oneto the netline
buckminster fuller would be envious
arrived in the digital world
the web is closed
the synapses are visible
private is a thing of the past;
there is no competition
whoever puts it on the web has won
the rest is a copy
silicon valley applauds
nyc is again the center of the projection
the projection of mars on earth
a paradise
a destination
a journey
once in a lifetime
no attack
handkerchief covering your face
because the spider in its web has programmed it that way
the danger is averted
the reserves can be invested
the cliff bears it with dignity
the systems are brought into line

culture
distraction
diversion
all are involved
nobody is excluded
everyone’s involved
nobody gets away
away from powerless!
ignore the skeptics!
everyone is affected
no one can escape
do nothing or something?
the climate doesn’t talk with us
act globally

deference is not personal

we
primo premio
our

town hall
buried hatchet

chamber
comrades

polis
network

but!
art is tenacious or faster
than time

a journey into the unknown

… a journey into the unknown certainty
one-way multiway indirect way walkway wrong way wayless way back
one-way now in colors and styles almost dumbfounded at being so unfounded
multiway in words and hope in familiar places
indirect way to sun-blessed warmth with additive
walkway all around and once more in dedication without coercion
wrong way to praise joy glimmer of hope mañana
wayless forever bridgeless encountered heart oppressed
way back with indirect way via southeast asia places small thoughts sunken,
words drunken
aroused covered scared, today tomorrow yesterday
the now

thou tirr dear
again and again constantly new

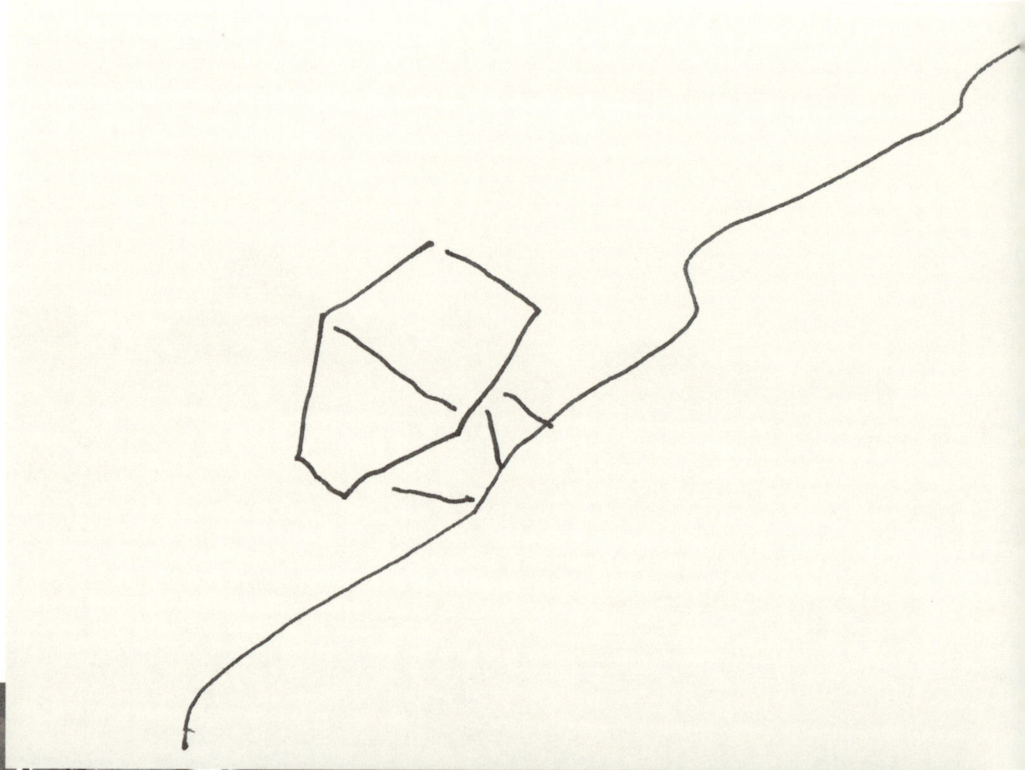

Guesthood

Time and again, a vain dull desire engenders in us an urge to establish distance to our neighbor by emphasizing differences and, in accordance with this mental image, to sort things into simple categories, namely into this and that.

When hubris, dynamic peer pressure, and an externally manipulated preservation instinct is added to the mix, playfulness leads to conflict—and what we then understand is: precisely nothing.

In one of his secondary works, *The Wisdom of Life*, within a section entitled "Fame," Schopenhauer quoted the great mathematician d'Alembert, who said: "the sanctuary of the temple is inhabited by the great dead, who during their life had no place there, and by a very few living persons, who are nearly all ejected on their death."

Guesthood—is that a state of being? It is. Is it a state of mind? We shall see. Who is the guest, the subject—a guest on Earth? A guest on Mother Earth. Mother Earth? Where is the father?

Fatherland.

The word is the history of the mother tongue, and the father is a technical impulse. Here we are on Mother Earth—as its guest. Each and every one of us is a guest.

Dreams, visions, and utopias are gifts for the illusion of having freedom of movement along the way. Air to breathe deeply. Physical contact in space. As much as possible, as big as possible, unlimited, parallel, colored, or better yet, colorful sounding, harmoniously coherent, and pleasant smelling. Floating and yet tethered within the fluid interior of the amniotic sac—or breathing but hardly able to move, bound to the Earth at the atmospheric exterior of the celestial body. It's all the same. We have lived and are living both states. Both are transitions. Both momentarily give rise in us to the trusting expectation of experiencing, extending, and stretching these temporary comforts. The body's circuitry, interacting with the physical sensors on its surface, contributes bit by bit—that is, from atom to atom—toward continually recreating its present, transient in the surf of time. A thin skin, translucent and capable of breathing. Not a protective film!

In interplay with all our senses, sensing or feeling the space in which we find ourselves makes it possible for us to be there for a moment. The other is always there: beyond.

"The arts of language owe their beauty to their proximity to that which resides outside language." (Michel Serres)

Reconstruction. Experiencing. Individual imprecisions are accepted. Growing up marveling, without words. Helpless. Life comes into being without any help from us. In a wondrous way, constantly and everywhere, even under the most adverse circumstances.

The fertilized egg cell makes itself at home, joins onto the great pulsating circulatory system, and seals itself off all around. The cells form, and bodily organs emerge. A head and a spinal column develop; a heart grows and begins to pump. The internal dynamics are at work. A connecting channel establishes a link. Two hearing organs and eardrums develop to provide orientation in space. Hands and feet take form to control the floating movement, the neck takes form to enable the head to turn independently of the rest. Genitalia begin to establish gender. The face takes shape. The neck becomes longer so that the head has more freedom of movement. The body has come into being. Fingers and toes separate at the extremities of the hands and feet. Movements of the mouth and touches by the fingers cause sucking reflexes. The proportions of the body change, vocal chords appear, eyebrows and hair grow, the facial muscles train and work actively, fluid expressions form as reactions to what goes on outside, and taste buds form on the tongue. The neck reaches full flexibility. The sexual organs are complete. The dimension of all this is not yet even as big as a fist. Ambient noises are perceived and selected, as are the activities of the adjacent organs, or voices and other sounds from outside. The lungs begin to work; fluid is transported in and back out. To protect from the cold later on, fatty tissue is formed as a cushion beneath the skin. Complete weightlessness: three-dimensional movement in space is now possible. New brain cells emerge continuously at an explosive rate, and downy hair grows over the entire body. As a test of digestion, the surrounding fluid is swallowed and then excreted via the urinary tract. There is a perception of temperature, pressure, pain, light, noise, and taste. Touch has become a sensory experience. A rhythm of sleeping and being awake brings time into play. Grasping movements and reflexes define and explore the surroundings. Sucking the thumb! Taste on the tongue. The production of white blood cells begins. Swallowing is practiced by drinking the amniotic fluid. The bone structure solidifies. The eyes are opened and closed; shapes, colors, and outlines become recognizable. The sleep–wake rhythm consolidates to become the body's inner clock. Movement exercises test the muscle contractions. All the sensory functions are working: hearing, touching, smelling, tasting, and seeing. One half of sleep is deep, the other half is REM. The skin becomes smoother. Space is getting tight; the brain develops fast. Noises are stored in memory. The space becomes ever tighter; the lanugo hair covering the body is shed and released into the amniotic fluid. The weight gains are enormous. All of the organs are now working in coordination, but still in trial mode. An entire whole.

All that remains now is to build up and store more fat deposits; nobody knows exactly what to expect. A release of hormones conveys a signal of readiness to take the first step on the journey to the next state of being.

The expulsion, initiated by the stimulating chemical composition, begins with irregular waves of pressure; the prelingual message is transported and communicated physically. With the back of the head first and the face downwards. The wave frequency increases, the pressure from behind becomes stronger, the preordained path opens up through the wall, and the amniotic sac bursts. The first cosmos is destroyed. The head emerges outside, accompanied by increased pressure and pulsating frequency. One turn, then the shoulders and the rest follow. Now comes shock in the face of a completely new situation, and the breathing function, already tested, bursts out abruptly, this time with air. It feels like nothing, much too light—now panic, sudden smells, skin on skin, direct contact; then the calming effect of the familiar heartbeat and, lightning-fast, freezing cold and with eyes closed ...

The umbilical cord is severed. The lingering sound of that sudden scream is louder than all the muffled sounds heard before.

The child's legal capacity as a person comes into full force the moment it leaves its mother's body.

Naked in a pleasantly temperate environment, quickly wrapped up in protective thermal packaging that conceals everything except the face and hands. Shell number one. Lucky for now.

This good fortune is owed to the place, the time, and the lovingly celebrated social ritual of those who are now the closest.

A new guest!

"Philosophy finds it an easy matter to vanquish past and future evils, but the present are commonly too hard for it." A maxim from François de La Rochefoucauld.

Being a guest.

Do we improve, respect, train, glorify, and transfigure our bodies because we are guest in them? Do we find ourselves in a society full of guests?

Mother Earth is our host, therefore the proprietor. Who is the guest? Strangers are guests. Strangers do not give up their camouflage. We know nothing of their origins or their intentions. Every one of us is a stranger. Looked at like a magical being on a catwalk—the fashion show—admired, revered, and downright glamorized by everyone. This is unfortunately of no use in everyday life, because the clothes fit no one. We refuse like defiant children to draw consequences from our self-destructive actions. All we do is bring forth strategies to calm the business-oriented conscience of this one-dimensional development.

Faced with the strategy of ever more and ever further, it helps to organize our thinking into boxes. Everyone to his own. Easy to stack and easy to manipulate. The objectives remain invisible within, hidden. Outwardly, everything can be additively stacked up and closed—an economically clear, comprehensible image.

"Economize!" is what we should efficaciously drill into young people's minds, economize and deal correctly with the delineated opportunities! After all, we must all find our way in the same system.

Thus: A necktie is compulsory, gentlemen; a man must stand up straight, buttoned to the neck. The shirt over the belly, the collar open. The button is closed. The tie is pulled through the artfully formed loop. Collar down, jacket on top.

How could it ever be different? The diver's penguin suit, the astronaut's bulbous head—every profession naturally comes up with its own special costume.

Black for priests and architects; sloppily creased attire for philosophers, scientists, and professors; too small and too tight for politicians (so that the head is unpleasantly emphasized); doctors in blue, whether striped or checked but in any case patterned; lawyers, civil servants, reporters, and businesspeople looking as if they'd just stepped out of a department store display; the police and military defining a formal frame of grayish-blue and green; and so on. Women dressed elegantly, men soberly. More or less colorful images emerge, like a stage backdrop that varies depending on the climate, customs, and society.

Our clothes enable us to set a superficial external sign bearing a message of our affiliation. Internationally, certain standardized items of clothing have become established throughout the First and Second Worlds. As a result, we are not able at first glance to distinguish between the guest and those who belong. For this reason, we are cautious and initially—because we are unsure—still speak of the guest, of the stranger with the unknown intentions. We must attempt to approach one another with all due hospitality, which might cause surprise and induce the other person to abandon the camouflage. But what happens when a guest is also the proprietor? In other words, when a guest is a host, and the stranger then ... what actually? We shouldn't just lump everything together, guest and host. But in order to look more closely at hospitality in our culture, we have to imagine that there must be someone who provides accommodation to the foreign guests; someone who feeds, entertains, understands, supervises, and cares for them, or maybe even jails and deports them. And, as if that weren't enough, we might have to adapt our house to the wishes of the unknown foreigner, change it accordingly, and give it a new orientation, a new alignment, without even having recognized the intentions. That's a dangerous game, presumably a trap we complacently fall into. It's enough to make you flip out! Since the whole topic is literally too much to endure, we should treat our guests with great care—especially if we think it through—because we could be guests ourselves at any time. Particularly when we compare the hospitality industry—where people earn money as hosts—with social hospitality—that is, the common good serving people's need for assistance—and examine them within the framework of our social perception in order to shed light, absolutely and comprehensively, on the meaning of hospitality.

Guesthood in the House of God. Refuge. Home. Spiritual hospitality. Amid the hustle and bustle, a place that we keep free from commercial interests is established as best we can; a place that aims for a greater good in what emanates from it, thus allowing the actuality of individual comings and goings to be ever-present. A this-worldly other world. Uncanny, cold, dire, and dark. Manifest. Light, material, scent, abstract peace. An inner conversation with a hoped-for future and thoughts of the past. The ritual process of charging these places is silently passed on from guest to guest, which is why the proprietors know everything.

That might also explain the incredible economic success of digital hospitality, where people eagerly and optimistically make their identities available in the form of data sets for "everyone" to use. From those, digital augmented realities can be derived without further ado—and although they do not actually play any role whatsoever in our individual experiences as guests, if humanity is a network-driven natural phenomenon, an overwhelmingly powerful proprietor could certainly conjure up with some ideas of what to do with our data. In short: We are currently experiencing a transformation from the Pantheon to the pandigital, and if we believe all the stories passed down to us, the will of the gods is uncontrollable.

The ritual of hospitality is an attitude toward strangers that has evolved in us over generations since the beginning of time: namely, to make a friend of the stranger or enemy, in an act of self-interest. Here, in exercising the action, we might formulate and acknowledge architecture as a framework for supporting and coping with this process on a regular basis. However, that would be only one possibility. Being a guest cannot be restricted solely to the pleasurable enjoyment of the Earth's surface, but must also be completely free in allowing the destruction and penetration of the same, at least in thought. Otherwise we will never go beyond our cribs, which must eventually be abandoned no matter what.

To overcome the hostile in the stranger, we must break through the surface, but what if the hostile stranger in ourselves is the strongest? Yes, what then? Being a guest, oscillating between guest and host. Gifts from a guest, give and take, what you give, I just take.

If only we didn't have that additional issue with harmony. We are constantly engaged in a vague pursuit of harmony. Everything around us must be harmonious and well balanced. We only have a hunch about where this need comes from; probably—as I have recognized in myself—from laziness, so as to avoid having to deal with chaotic circumstances and continually having to come up with new ideas, or from the fear of being in an uncertain state in which perhaps no new ideas come to mind. Nevertheless, over and over again we are surprised at the perseverance that our endeavor to keep everything in well-balanced harmony demands of us as a matter of course, even when it results in a condition of standstill.

At the core is the cozy circle of habit. Every dissonance immediately upsets everything; every stumbling block demands prompt removal, every unevenness needs straightening, every instance of contamination requires remedial action. Bearing this in mind, the challenge for an avant-garde was and always is to be an uncomfortable irritant. That's easily said but a difficult fate, because at present it's hardly possible to win over any support. This means the activity that brings with it the rudiments of renewal is mostly an unprofitable undertaking and, beyond that, only recognizable for those in the know. There are always exceptions when the time is right, but that is something none of us realize until later, when it is too late. The guests are the strangers. The foreign has its own story.

Back to the origins, but this time let's move ahead progressively with an always-know-it-all mentality. Every blackbird sings, as does every blue whale—and in addition, perhaps a mole, blind and mute, ploughs the soil so the air gains momentum on the land. Knowing nothing of the fact that no one can escape these truths, and once again we have a problem that does not exist—because all problems are homemade; they are products of our own making. The world is not harmonious and therefore knows no problem with harmony. Everything is in sync. Only a human being could think up such nonsense. The human problem will perhaps be resolved, or more accurately, will solve itself. Nature doesn't give a damn whether we adapt our way of thinking to reality or not. Nature does not think about us at all. Even though we are the guests.

We have coaxed more than one or two secrets out of nature, and have also deciphered, discovered, and decoded a great deal; we've developed and computed technical codes. Much of it works, much of it backfires; we know how certain things work, but we don't know why.

"There are and can be but two opinions; for Nature is either the offspring ... of the Divine Word ... or else of the seeds of things mixed and confused together." (Francis Bacon)

The rigid mummies have left behind pyramids and sarcophagi made of granite, an eloquent testament of our lasting existence as guests even after death, whose book we can read but not fully understand. Necropolises, cemeteries, and ancestral portrait galleries are legacies of past cultures that hospitably place the precursory knowledge of the ancients at our disposal. In archaeological excavations we seek the traces of lives once lived so we can try to make sense of what life once was. When we, as guests, sneak away from the planet one day, what remains will initially be radioactive substances and plastic. For reasons of sentimentality, we should give thought to what the ancient dictum says about inheritance: Après nous, le déluge. It is a credo of hospitality we proffer to those who come after us. For Abraham, hospitality was the future. But we take the easy path. Clothed in the humanistic skin of our ancestors. Side-by-side, we hear ourselves in the primordial soup. Dull, wave-like, oppressive, tugging tension and release. Impulse and desire maintain the forces that oppose nature.

Two central questions arise, even if an answer seems to be as simple as it is senseless. Nevertheless, they are at least like a mirror on the wall that can be consulted before arriving as a guest in the neighbor's garden.

Why does having an abundance of children go hand-in-hand with poverty?

Why is it that in our society, bad guys are worshipped instead of gods?

"The strangers are coming!" shouts the child upon seeing arriving guests. Adopted from Roman law, we subconsciously understand that conceding the right to hospitality is dangerous; strangers as guests might also harbor hostile intentions.

We live out our history as continual technical and scientific progress—and the newly found comes on top of that. Are we making the same progress with those who have newly joined us as participants?

Is our architecture an architecture of hospitality, or are we too wrapped up in ourselves and therefore too preoccupied with exclusion? Georg Driendl

"Why complain about enemies?
Could those become your friends —
To whom your very existence —
Is an eternal silent reproach?"

Goethe

Category	Project	Commisioner	Type	City	Period	Status
Restaurant/Bar	Skala Bar & Restaurant	Gastronomiebetriebs- und Kulturveranst. GmbH	direct	Vienna	1987	built
Residential	Standard Solar	Private	direct	Langenrohr	1987–1989	built
School	*School for Visually Impaired Children	City of Vienna	direct	Vienna	1992–1995	built
Residential	Solar Skeleton	Private	direct	Mieders	1995–1996	built
Pedestrian Bridge	*Bridge over the Kamp	Private	direct	Buchberg	1996	unbuilt
Urban Design	Am Lohbach	NHT	int'l competition, 2nd prize	Innsbruck	1996	unbuilt
School	Blumauergasse School Complex	City of Vienna	Expert assessment	Vienna	1997	unbuilt
Residential	Solar Cube	Private	direct	Vienna	1997	built
Residential	Satellite Beach	NHT	competition, 1st prize	Innsbruck	1997–2003	built
School	*Atrium School	City of Vienna	competition	Vienna	1998	unbuilt
Residential	Solar Atrium	Private	direct	Breitenfurt	1998	built
Residential	Solar Shift	Private	direct	Vienna	1998	built
Exhibition	*Conflict and Culture	Sigmund Freud Society	direct	Vienna	1998–1999	built
School	*Austrian School Budapest	Federal Ministry of Education, Science and Culture	competition, 1st prize	Budapest	1998–2001	built
Residential	Citygate	NHT	competition, 1st prize	Innsbruck	1998–2003	built
Residential	Solar Tube	Private	direct	Vienna	1999–2001	built
Residential	TE 13	NHT	direct	Telfs	1999–2002	built
Office	*Twist Tower TT 5	Kallco Construct	direct	Vienna	2000–2002	built
Office	Biotop Headquarters	Biotop GmbH	competition	Weidling	2001	unbuilt
Residential	TR 01	NHT	direct	Trins	2001–2004	built
Exhibition	Deanimated	Kunsthalle Wien	direct	Vienna	2002	built
Tourism	Austria Pavilion	–	competition	St. Moritz	2002	unbuilt
Landmark	*Ground Zero	d*a	self-initiative	New York	2002	unbuilt
Residential	TE 15	BauArt Immobilien GmbH	direct	Telfs	2002–2003	built
Residential	Solar Box	Private	direct	Vienna	2002–2003	built
Residential	Solar Deck	Private	direct	Vienna	2002–2003	built
Residential	Solar Mount	Private	direct	Vienna	2002–2003	built
Hotel	Shape Deck	MAK	invited contribution	Los Angeles	2003	unbuilt
Hotel	*Lux Alpinae	Private	direct	St. Anton am Arlberg	2003	built
Exhibition	Friedrich Kiesler Foundation	Kiesler Stiftung Wien	direct	Vienna	2004	built
Residential	Senior and Starter Homes	NHT	invited competition, 1st prizeinvited competition, 1st place	Kufstein	2004–2006	built
Restaurant/Bar	*Orient Occident	Keskin OG	direct	Vienna	2004–2007	built
Office	*European Patent Office	European Patent Office	competition, 1st prize	Vienna	2004–	ongoing
Office	*Office 2	d*a	self-initiative	Vienna	2005	built
Cable Car Station	*Galzigbahn Valley Station	Arlberger Bergbahnen AG	competition, 1st prize	St. Anton am Arlberg	2005–2006	built
Museum	*Klosterneuburg Monastery Museum	Stift Klosterneuburg	competition, 1st prize	Klosterneuburg	2005–2006	built
Museum	Hunting Museum	Landesmuseum Joanneum	competition, 1st prize	Stainz	2005–2006	built
Residential	am Lohbach	Innsbrucker Stadtbau GmbH	competition, 1st prize	Innsbruck	2005–2008	built

Museum	*Forchtenstein Castle	Burg Forchtenstein Kulturverwaltungs GmbH	direct	Forchtenstein	2005–	ongoing
Interior	*Office	Private	direct	Vienna	2006	built
Hotel	*5-Star Hotel	Riemergasse 7 Entwicklungs-und Verwertungs GmbH	direct	Vienna	2006	unbuilt
Headquarters	*ThyssenKrupp Quarter	Thyssen Krupp AG	int'l competition	Essen	2006	unbuilt
Urban Design	*Almaty Urban Development Plan	Deutsche Planbau GmbH	direct	Almaty	2006	unbuilt
Entertainment	Donau Park	Union of Kurdistan	direct	Sulaimaniyya	2006	unbuilt
Residential	Cubic Lights	Private	direct	Vienna	2006–2008	built
Residential	Palais Cité	Riemergasse 2 Besitzgesellschaft mbH	direct	Vienna	2006–2010	built
Multiuse	*B26 Office Tower	UNIQA Real Estate AG	direct	Belgrade	2007	unbuilt
Tourism	*Mogren Hill Montenegro	Raiffeisen Evolution	direct	Montenegro	2007	unbuilt
Tourism	*Mogren Garden Montenegro	Raiffeisen Evolution	direct	Montenegro	2007	unbuilt
Office	*Kurtsan Headquarters	Kurtsan Holding	direct	Istanbul	2007	unbuilt
Residential Development	*Solar Standard Kotowo	RiGroup	competition, 1st prize	Kotowo	2007	unbuilt
Urban Design	*Hoverfront Dublin	The Chicago Athenaeum	invited contribution	Dublin	2007	unbuilt
Interior	*Doctor's Office	Private	direct	Vienna	2007	built
Residential	Apartment Building	Private	direct	Mieming	2007	built
Museum	Nature Park Museum	Marktgemeinde Kaindorf an der Sulm KG	direct	Kaindorf an der Sulm	2007–2009	built
Museum	Agriculture Museum	Landesmuseum Joanneum GmbH	direct	Stainz	2007–2009	built
Residential	Apartment Building	Private	direct	Völkermarkt	2007–2010	built
Residential	Assisted Living	NHT	competition	Zirl	2007–2010	built
Hotel	*7-Star Hotel	Seven Stars Galleria	direct	Istanbul	2008	unbuilt
Sports	*Olympic Village for YOG 2012	NHT	direct	Innsbruck	2008	built
Bridge	*Metro West Liffey Bridge	Railway Procurement Agency	int'l competition	Liffey	2008	unbuilt
Interior	Doctor's Office	Private	direct	Innsbruck	2008	built
Office	*Infill	Private	direct	Vienna	2008	unbuilt
Multiuse	*ITC Sofia	Link AD	direct	Sofia	2008	unbuilt
Interior	Gallery	Art Sümer	direct	Istanbul	2008	built
Laboratory	*Mobile Lab	Kurtsan Holding	direct	Bodrum	2008	unbuilt
Pedestrian Bridge	River Douglas Bridge	Lancashire County Council	competition	Lancashire	2008	unbuilt
Office	*Waagner-Biro Headquarters	Columbus Immobilien	competition	Vienna	2008	unbuilt
Tunnel Portal	*Daylight Converter	Arriyadh Development Authority	study	Riyadh	2008	unbuilt
Cable Car Station	*Rendlbahn Valley Station	Arlberger Bergbahnen AG	direct	St. Anton am Arlberg	2008–2009	built
Bus Terminal	*Transport Hub	Arlberger Bergbahnen AG	direct	St. Anton am Arlberg	2008–2009	built
Pedestrian Bridge	*Valley Connection	Arlberger Bergbahnen AG	direct	St. Anton am Arlberg	2008–2009	built
Museum	*Topkapi Master Plan	d*a	self-initiative	Istanbul	2008–2014	unbuilt
Residential	WÖ 12 & WÖ 23	NHT	direct	Wörgl	2008–2015	built
Laboratory	*Laboratory Building	Herbafarm	direct	Bodrum	2009	built
Landmark	*Origin	d*a	self-initiative		2009	unbuilt
Traffic	*Traffic Control	Arriyadh Development Authority	direct	Riyadh	2009	unbuilt
Multiuse	*Master Plan	Bruneckerstraße Ost GmbH	competition	Innsbruck	2009	unbuilt
Residential	Apartment Building	Private	direct	Frankfurt	2009	built

Pedestrian Bridge	*Connecting Link	Vienna Municipal Administration	int'l competition	Vienna	2009	unbuilt
Cable Car Station	*Ifinger Cableway	Ifinger Seilbahnen AG	competition	Meran	2009	unbuilt
Landmark	*Perpa	d*a	self-initiative	Istanbul	2009	unbuilt
Museum	House of Arts and Culture	Lebanese Ministry of Culture	int'l competition	Beirut	2009	unbuilt
Industrial	Winery Press Building	Stift Klosterneuburg	direct	Klosterneuburg	2009–2010	built
Residential	Apartment Building	Private	direct	Unterretzbach	2009–2011	built
Sports	*Vienna Indoor Swimming Pool	Wiener Stadthalle Betriebs- und Veranstaltungsges. m.b.H.	int'l competition, 1st prize	Vienna	2009–2015	built
Office	*Office 3	d*a	self-initiative	Mieders	2009–	ongoing
Residential Development	Desert Green	A. Richter	direct	Parndorf	2009–	ongoing
Museum	*Highlights, Haydnsaal	F.E.Familien-Privatstiftung Eisenstadt	direct	Eisenstadt	2010	built
Museum	*Treasure Chamber	Stift Klosterneuburg	int'l competition, 1st prize	Klosterneuburg	2010–2011	built
Landmark	*Restaurant, Gallery	VERBUND Tourismus GmbH	competition, 2nd prize	Schlegeis	2011	unbuilt
Sports	Skater Hall	IIG	direct	Innsbruck	2011	built
Sports	*Sports Center and Climbing Hall	IIG	study	Innsbruck	2011	unbuilt
Cable Car Station	*Vallugabahn	Arlberger Bergbahnen AG	study	St. Anton am Arlberg	2011	unbuilt
Restaurant/Bar	*Zweitbester Restaurant & Bar	Zweitbester GmbH	direct	Vienna	2011	built
School	*Liese Prokop Private School	ÖLSZ	competition	Maria Enzersdorf	2011	unbuilt
Museum	*Apartment of the Princess in Esterházy Palace	F.E.Familien-Privatstiftung Eisenstadt	direct	Eisenstadt	2011–2012	built
Residential	Residential Development	NHT	competition, 1st prize	Lienz	2011–	ongoing
School	Media Center	Bundesimmobiliengesellschaft m.b.H.	competition	Vienna	2012	unbuilt
Market	*Falcon Market, Riyadh	Arriyadh Development Authority	study	Riyadh	2012	unbuilt
Residential	City Loft	Private	direct	Vienna	2012	built
Museum	Falconry Gallery, Neue Burg Palace	Kunsthistorisches Museum Wien	direct	Vienna	2012–2013	built
Cable Car Station	*Kappl Cable Car Station	Bergbahnen Kappl GmbH & CoKG	competition, 3rd prize	Kappl	2012–2013	unbuilt
Royal Palace	House of Gazelle	Gazelle	direct	South Africa	2012–	ongoing
Sports	Two Steps to the Stadium	d*a	self-initiative		2013	unbuilt
Urban Design	*"Oasis31" Climate Shell	Private	self-initiative	Fudschaira	2013	unbuilt
Museum	*Contemporary Art Museum	NCCA	int'l competition	Moscow	2013	unbuilt
School	*Comprehensive School Concept for St. Leonhard	NHT	direct	St. Leonhard	2013–2014	unbuilt
Bridges	*KAR Interchange Road Design	Arriyadh Development Authority	direct	Riyadh	2013–2015	built
Tunnel	*KAR Interchange Road Design	Arriyadh Development Authority	direct	Riyadh	2013–2015	built
Residential	Apartment Building	NHT	direct	St. Leonhard	2013–2015	built
Landmark	*Light Balls	Arriyadh Development Authority	direct	Riyadh	2013–2017	ongoing
Cable Car Station	*Mühlbach Modern	Gitschberg Jochtal AG	selection process, 1st prize	Mühlbach	2013–	ongoing
Residential	New Start Homes	NHT	direct	Unterperfuss	2013–	ongoing
School	*IST Administration Building	IST Austria	competition	Gugging	2014	unbuilt
Concert House	*House of Music	IIG	competition	Innsbruck	2014	unbuilt
Trade Fair	*Convention Center	CP Beijing	int'l invited contribution	Nanjing	2014	unbuilt
Residential	Apartment Building	NHT	direct	Vomp	2014–2015	built
Pedestrian Bridge	*St. Corona Children's Sports World	Bergbahnen St. Corona GmbH	direct	St. Corona	2014–2016	built

Multiuse	*St. Corona Children's Sports World	Bergbahnen St. Corona GmbH	direct	St. Corona	2014–2016	built
Sports	Ice Hockey Stadium	NHT	direct/study	Lienz	2014–	ongoing
Residential	Haus des Lebens (Assisted Living)	NHT	direct	St. Anton am Arlberg	2014–2017	ongoing
Residential	Residential Development	NHT	direct	Oberndorf	2014–	ongoing
Residential Development	Smart Living Breitenlee	Immobilien Vorsorge GmbH	direct	Vienna	2014–	ongoing
Entertainment	*Entertainment Park	Apolo Ampex	direct	Lahore	2014–	ongoing
Museum	*Vienna Museum	Wien Museum Projekt GmbH	competition	Vienna	2015	unbuilt
School	*Elementary School	NHT	competition	Mieders	2015	unbuilt
Urban Design	*Neu Marx	Immobilienentwicklungs GmbH	direct	Vienna	2015	unbuilt
Residential	Apartment Building	NHT	direct	Fließ	2015–2017	built
Residential	Apartment Building	Private	direct	Vienna	2015–2017	built
Residential	Apartment Building	NHT	direct	Fließ	2015–	ongoing
School	*MCI	State of Tyrol	int'l competition	Innsbruck	2016	unbuilt
Urban Design	*City District	State of Lower Austria	invited contribution	Wiener Neustadt	2016	unbuilt
Student Housing	*Karstadt	gewobau Rüsselsheim mbH	invited contribution	Rüsselsheim	2016–	ongoing
Office	Google Headquarters	d*a	self-initiative	New York	2016–	ongoing
Hotel	*4-Star Hotel	Private	selection process, 1st prize	Mühlbach	2016–	ongoing
Urban Design	*City District and Park	CC Vienna Invest GmbH	int'l competition, 1st prize	Vienna	2016–	ongoing
Open-Air Museum	*Weg über den Berg	F.E.Familien-Privatstiftung Eisenstadt	direct	St. Margarethen	2016–	ongoing
Residential	New Start Homes	NHT	study	Rum	2016–	ongoing
Residential	New Start Homes	NHT	study	Umhausen	2016–	ongoing
Residential	Residential Development	NHT	direct	Rum	2016–	ongoing
Residential	New Start Homes	NHT	study	Lienz	2017–	ongoing
Religious building	*Wedding Chapel	Domänen Privatstiftung	direct	Lackenbach	2017–	ongoing
Hotel	Guest house	Stift Klosterneuburg	direct	Klosterneuburg	2017–	ongoing
Residential	Apartment Building	NHT	direct	Jenbach	2017–	ongoing
Museum	Nature Park Museum	Jurmala City Council	int'l competition	Riga	2017–	unbuilt
Restaurant/Bar	Bar Luster	Zweitbester GmbH	direct	Vienna	2017–	built
School	Education Campus	Russian International School	direct	Bruck an der Leitha	2017–	ongoing
Residential	New Start Homes	NHT	direct	Baumkirchen	2017–	ongoing
Residential	New Start Homes	NHT	direct	Haiming	2017–	ongoing
Residential	Apartment	Private	direct	Vienna	2017–	ongoing
Residential	Residential Development	NHT	study	Seefeld	2017–	ongoing
Residential	New Start Homes	NHT	study	Gries im Sellrain	2017–	ongoing
Residential	New Start Homes	NHT	study	Inzing	2017–	ongoing
Residential	Apartment Building	Private	direct	Vienna	2017–	ongoing
Cable Car Station	Metroférico	INONERIDE/ILF/Doppelmayr	direct	Quito	2017–	ongoing
Pedestrian Bridge	Wadi As Sulai	Arriyadh Development Authority	direct	Riyadh	2017–	ongoing

Projects marked with an asterisk * are found in this book.
Our residential projects have already been extensively presented in the book
APop living (Vienna / New York: Springer, 2010).

Index

ITC Sofia
rendering driendl*architects, 2008, p. 215, 299

Jewish Museum Vienna
plans Georg Driendl (driendl*steixner), 1990er, p. 16, 23

Kappl Cable Car Station
rendering driendl*architects, 2013/2017, p. 141, 142–143

Klosterneuburg Monastery Museum
photo Georg Driendl, 2012, p. 317
photos Lew Rodin, 2008, p. 96, 97, 98;
2009, 158, 166; 2014, p. 354
photos Milli Kaufmann, 2006, p. 350–351;
2010, p. 97, 315; 2011, p. 99
photos Roland Krauss, 2006, p. 163, 203
photos James Morris, 2017, p. 164, 165, 167, 169, 367
Pläne driendl*architects, 2005, p. 167; 2013, p. 355

Liese Prokop Private School
rendering driendl*architects, 2011, p. 212

Light Balls
rendering driendl*architects, 2015/2017, p. 101, 256, 260–261

Lipizzaner
photo Georg Driendl, 2014, p. 283

Master Plan
photo Milli Kaufmann, 2011, p. 241 b.
rendering driendl*architects, 2010, p. 204–205

MCI
rendering driendl*architects, 2016, p. 174

Media School
rendering driendl*architects, 2012, p. 124

Metro West Liffey Bridge
photo Milli Kaufmann, 2011, p. 235 b.
Pläne driendl*architects, 2008, p. 285, 292–293
rendering driendl*architects, 2008/2017, p. 11, 290–291

Mobile Lab
rendering driendl*architects, 2007, p. 136

Mobile Paradise
photo Milli Kaufmann, 2011, p. 237 a.
rendering driendl*architects, 2007, p. 182–183

Model Title
Ursula Aichwalder, Andrea Driendl, Georg Driendl,
2015/2016, p. 235–243

Mogren Garden
rendering driendl*architects, 2007, p. 327, 328

Mogren Hill
photo Milli Kaufmann, 2011, p. 240 b.
rendering driendl*architects, 2007, p. 327

Mühlbach Modern
rendering driendl*architects, 2018, p. 132–133

Neu Marx
plans driendl*architects, 2015, p. 135

NYC
photo driendl*architects, 2002, p. 206

“Oasis 31” Climate Shell
rendering driendl*architects, 2013, p. 57, 62
plan driendl*architects, 2013, p. 262

Office
photo Milli Kaufmann, 2009, p. 52 a.

Office 1
photo driendl*architects, 2009, p. 10

Office 2
photos Milli Kaufmann, 2007, p. 12, 14, 300;
2011, p. 17; 2014, p. 22; 2018, p. 13
photo James Morris, 2017, p. 297

Office 3
photos Georg Driendl, 2010, p. 68; 2011, p. 12
photo driendl*architects, 2010, p. 320
photo Lew Rodin, 2013, p. 321
photos Milli Kaufmann, 2015, p. 21, 69

Office Tower B 26
photo Milli Kaufamnn, 2011, p. 239
rendering driendl*architects, 2007, p. 213

Olympic Village for YOG 2012
rendering driendl*architects, 2008/2018, p. 252

Orient Occident
photos Milli Kaufmann, 2007, p. 178, 181, 185, 187

Origin
photo Milli Kaufamnn, 2011, p. 236 a.

Perpa
plan driendl*architects, 2012, p. 196–198
rendering driendl*architects, 2012/2017, p. 118 a., 124

Picture Puzzle Gull
photo Georg Driendl, 2017, p. 244–245

Poems
Ursula Aichwalder, p. 107–108

Andrea Driendl, p. 7, 10, 15 r., 16, 22, 99, 101,
107–108, 122, 140, 160, 184, 213, 244–245, 257, 258,
286, 301, 321, 330, 348, 364, 366
Georg Driendl, p. 7, 15 l., 20, 29, 32, 34, 38, 50, 58,
85, 126, 142, 179, 186, 206, 217,
220, 223, 283, 295, 315, 316, 352, 353, 357, 358
Kathrin Turanitz, p. 46, 324

Q Train
photo Milli Kaufamnn, 2011, p. 243
rendering driendl*architects, 2003, p. 207

Rendlbahn Valley Station
photo Lew Rodin, 2009, p. 131
photos Milli Kaufmann, 2009, p. 137; 2010, p. 128
plan driendl*architects, 2009, p. 130, 140, 222

Restaurant, Gallery
rendering driendl*architects, 2011, p. 268 a., 269

School for Visually Impaired Children
photos James Morris, 2002, p. 46, 48–49, 51

SETE France
Pläne Georg Driendl (driendl*steixner), 1990er, p. 56, 63, 134

Shape Deck
photo Joshua White, 2005, p. 238 b.
rendering driendl*architects, 2003, p. 293

Sigmund Freud Society/Conflict and Culture
photo James Morris, 2003, p. 34–35
photo driendl*architects, 2003, p. 257

Skala Bar & Restaurant
photos James Morris, 2009, p. 258, 259

Skatchy
Clear to Circus, Georg Driendl, 1998, p. 4, 9
Untitled, Georg Driendl, 2002, p. 296
Untitled, Georg Driendl, 2006, p. 93
Genetically Modified Architecture, Georg Driendl, 2011, p. 248
iHouse, Georg Driendl, 2013, p. 20
Untitled, Georg Driendl, 2015, p. 366, p. 171
Artist in Motion, Georg Driendl, 2016, p. 56
Untitled, Georg Driendl, 2016, p. 29, 69, 99, 141, 223,
212, 301, 259, 269, 330, 358
Untitled, Georg Driendl, 2017, p. 15, 82, 137, 157, 165,
182, 184, 220, 252, 287, 264, 318, 321, 348

Sports Center and Climbing Hall
rendering driendl*architects, 2011, p. 251

St. Corona Children’s Sports World
photo Georg Driendl, 2016, p. 7

photo driendl*architects, 2016, p. 180
photo Milli Kaufamnn, 2016, p. 186

St. Leonhard School
Rendendering driendl*architects, 2015, p. 322

Student Housing
rendering driendl*architects, 2016/2017, p. 224

Topkapi Master Plan
plan driendl*architects, 2009, p. 218–219
rendering driendl*architects, 2010, p. 219

Traffic Control Riyadh
photo Milli Kaufmann, 2011, p. 238 a.

Trinity
rendering driendl*architects, 2006, p. 178, 213, 267
plan driendl*architects, 2006, p. 90–91

Twist Tower TT5
photos James Morris, 2002, p. 79, 83, 199, 200
Pläne driendl*architects, 2001, p. 160, 299

Untitled Images
Georg Driendl, 2010, p. 280; 2011, p. 326; 2014, p. 314, 318–319; 2017, p. 329

Vienna Indoor Swimming Pool
photo Milli Kaufmann, 2016, p. 89
photos James Morris, 2017, p. 80–81, 85, 86–87, 90–91, 104, 106, 108–109
plan driendl*architects, 2010, p. 88

Vienna Museum
rendering driendl*architects, 2015, p. 352, 356–357

Waagner-Biro Headquarters
rendering driendl*architects, 2008, p. 82

Wedding Chapel
photo driendl*architects, 2017, p. 325
rendering driendl*architects, 2017/2018, p. 346, 349

Weg über den Berg
photo Georg Driendl, 2016, p. 30
photos Milli Kaufmann, 2017, p. 306, 309
plan driendl*architects, 2017, p. 31
rendering driendl*architects, 2017, p. 176–177, 364–365

Zweitbester Restaurant & Bar
photos Milli Kaufmann, 2016, p. 52 b., 64
photo James Morris, 2017, p. 264
plan driendl*architects, 2016, p. 65

Acknowledgments

Our very special thanks go to all our collaborators and to all those who place their trust in us.

We are grateful to Christof Nardin for the graphic concept of this book, for guiding us along a wonderful path through the material jungle, and for the title.

Our thanks go to our copyeditor, Esther Pirchner, for her adept editing of the original texts and to David Koralek for the consummate English translation.

Thanks also extend to Lindsay Jane Munro for the English copyediting and to Graeme Morgan, who has likewise read the English texts. Appreciation also goes to Julia Spengler for sharing initial remarks to our texts.

We also express sincere thanks to Ursula Aichwalder, who has given us tireless inspiration to make this book, and to Eva Guttmann of Park Books, who has supported us from the beginning, advised us, and always believed that our efforts will succeed.

Sponsored by tirol Unser Land

Colophon

Editor: Georg Driendl

Co-Editor: Franz Driendl

Authors: Georg Driendl, Franz Driendl
Andrea Driendl, Kathrin Turanitz, Ursula Aichwalder

Project management: Kathrin Turanitz

Design: Bueronardin

Image editing: Milli Kaufmann
in cooperation with Ursula Aichwalder

Translation: David Koralek, ArchiTrans

Copy editing (German): Esther Pirchner

Proofreading (English): Lindsay Jane Munro

Production: Book Print Manfred Kleisel

Paper: Munken Kristall Rough

Park Books
Niederdorfstrasse 54, 8001 Zurich, Switzerland
www.park-books.com

Park Books is being supported by the Federal Office of Culture with a general subsidy for the years 2016–2020.

English edition: ISBN 978-3-03860-120-3
German edition: ISBN 978-3-03860-119-7